The Axiology of Friedrich Nietzsche

Nicolae Râmbu

The Axiology of
Friedrich Nietzsche

PETER LANG
EDITION

Bibliographic Information published by the Deutsche Nationalbibliothek
The Deutsche Nationalbibliothek lists this publication in the Deutsche Nationalbibliografie; detailed bibliographic data is available in the internet at http://dnb.d-nb.de.

Library of Congress Cataloging-in-Publication Data
Names: Râmbu, Nicolae, author.
Title: The axiology of Friedrich Nietzsche / Nicolae Râmbu.
Description: 1 [edition]. | New York : Peter Lang, 2016. | Includes bibliographical references.
Identifiers: LCCN 2016024318 | ISBN 9783631676387
Subjects: LCSH: Nietzsche, Friedrich Wilhelm, 1844-1900. | Values.
Classification: LCC B3318.V25 R36 2016 | DDC 193--dc23 LC record available at https://lccn.loc.gov/2016024318

This work was supported by a grant of the Romanian National Authority for Scientific Research and Innovation, CCCDI – UEFISCDI, project number 17/2016, Heritage Plus – HeAT, within PNCDI III.

ISBN 978-3-631-67638-7 (Print)
E-ISBN 978-3-653-07019-4 (E-Book)
DOI 10.3726/978-3-653-07019-4

© Peter Lang GmbH
Internationaler Verlag der Wissenschaften
Frankfurt am Main 2016
All rights reserved.
Peter Lang Edition is an Imprint of Peter Lang GmbH.

Peter Lang – Frankfurt am Main · Bern · Bruxelles · New York · Oxford · Warszawa · Wien

This publication has been peer reviewed.

www.peterlang.com

Contents

Preface

Despite a rich literature dedicated to the philosophy of Friedrich Nietzsche, research on his axiology is still in its early stages. It is obvious that he did not develop a general theory of values, but it can be extracted with sufficient precision from his literary-philosophical discourse, because *value* is the preferred object of the philosophical reflections in all his work.

In his unmistakable style, Friedrich Nietzsche approached the issue of all classes of values, not only the moral ones. Vital and economic values, religious and political values, moral and aesthetic values and, in addition to all these, value in general, with all its implications for human life and humanity, became one by one the object of reflections so profound that it can be said that Friedrich Nietzsche was undoubtedly a philosopher of values *par excellence*. He had an instinct for value, a faculty for feeling the finest nuances of the phenomenon of value and a passion for knowing the axiological universe that were so extraordinary they have rarely been seen in the history of culture.

In this paper, I tried to a certain extent to apply Friedrich Nietzsche's method to himself; I tried to be myself in relation to his work, a "*subterrestrial* at work, digging, mining, undermining", as he said himself in the *Preface* of *The Dawn of Day*. Anyone who has the patience to read him *lento* and to dig inside his work and personality will still have much to discover. *The Axiology of Friedrich Nietzsche* is an attempt to highlight some unique aspects of a writer of whom it can be said, paradoxically, that the more you study him, the more unknown he seems.

I. The Revaluation of all Values

1. The origin of values

Although he referred mainly to moral and religious values, Friedrich Nietzsche had in mind the entire axiological spectrum throughout his work. Typically, he meant by morality (*Moral*) a whole system of values, not only moral values in the strict sense of the word. Aesthetic values, theoretical values, economic values and other categories of values were, one by one, objects of reflection for an author who had without doubt a major role in the emergence of axiology as a general theory of values.

The problem of the origin of values is addressed in particular in *On the Genealogy of Morals*, but it is present episodically in most of the rest of his work. Friedrich Nietzsche's thesis about the origin of spiritual values is well known: the highest values and ideals of humanity have their roots in the lower layers of human beings. Everything that is sublime comes from a terrible misery. Masterpieces, as things carrying spiritual values, originate from the beastly layers of the human being. Plato, for instance, "says, with an innocence for which one must be Greek and not 'Christian', that there would be no Platonic philosophy at all if Athens had not possessed such beautiful youths: it was the sight of them which first plunged the philosopher's soul into an erotic whirl and allowed it no rest until it had implanted the seed of all high things into so beautiful a soil".[1]

It is not only morality, in the strict sense of the term, but also all types of spiritual values that are simple masks by which man hides his basest instincts. This idea of Friedrich Nietzsche's about the origin of values and especially moral values is not original; on the contrary, it was extensively circulated at that time by some "English psychologists", despite the fact that he began the *First Essay* in *On the Genealogy of Morals* by combating them. Also, modern materialism and positivism were the inspiration for his conception of the origin of values. Friedrich Nietzsche's contribution consisted in emphasizing the relative character of any moral and highlighting the fact

---

1 Friedrich Nietzsche, *Twilight of the Idols*, Penguin Books, New York, 2003, pp. 91–92.

that its origins are always suspect. In the *Observation* of the end of the *First Essay*, he raised a very subtle axiological problem, namely that "of the *value of previous evaluations*",[2] which also means implicitly putting the question of the evaluator's value. And, given that "there is no such thing as moral phenomena, but only a moral interpretation of phenomena",[3] the problem of *hermeneutic equity* becomes capital in Friedrich Nietzsche's axiology. He realized that neither the anthropological, historical and psychological information of that day nor his philological speculations were sufficient to provide a satisfactory answer to the question of the origin of values. This is why he made an appeal, quite unusual for his style, to the faculties of philology to promote historical study of morality and to collaborate with specialists in other fields to tackle this problem. "From now on, *all* disciplines have to prepare the future task of the philosophers: this task being understood as the solution of the *problem of value*, the determination of the hierarchy of values".[4]

What seems to have been firmly established by Nietzsche himself about the birth of values is that they have dubious origins and that, despite their apparent brightness, values feed on a *swamp*, as he said in *On the Genealogy of Morals*. And yet, values would not lose their validity even if their miserable origin could be demonstrated with mathematical rigour. Could anyone challenge the beauty of the water lily just because it has its roots in a *swamp*? This observation was made as early as 1905, by Giovanni Papini in his paper *The Twilight of the Philosophers*.

Friedrich Nietzsche's frequent use of the term *Instinkt* and its derivatives to explain the origin of moral values led to his characterization as Darwinian. As is well known, he protested vehemently when he was considered idealistic. In Friedrich Nietzsche's axiology, *instinct*, in the sense of animal impulse, as opposed to reason, plays no role. Unfortunately, he was not a theoretician and he never defined his terms, but he was always very attentive to context. The word itself has no meaning, but it receives one in a

---

2   Friedrich Nietzsche, *On the Genealogy of Morals*, Oxford University Press, 2008, p. 37.
3   Friedrich Nietzsche, *Beyond Good and Evil*, available at https://www.gutenberg. org/ebooks/4363. Accessed February 28, 2016.
4   Friedrich Nietzsche, *On the Genealogy of Morals*, p. 38.

certain context. This is the lesson well taken up by Nietzsche from Schleiermacher and other eminent German philologists of that era. In this case, *Instinkt* has a biological significance, preserved to this day in German and most European languages, but for Friedrich Nietzsche, and not only him, this term has a completely different meaning. When it came to spiritual values, Friedrich Nietzsche used the term *Instinkt* in the same way that, later, the German authors making serious contributions in axiology, such as Max Scheler and Nicolai Hartmann, used the term *Wertgefühl*. Therefore, it is about the faculty of man to feel, to intuit or to comprise values. Furthermore, reason has no power over them, because values belong to the emotional side of the human spirit.

It is not fair to say that, for Nietzsche, "the instincts are sacred"[5] without specifying the context in which *instinct* is present and which, as stated above, substitutes for definition of the concept. It is obvious that many confusions and misinterpretations appear this way. By *Instinkt*, Friedrich Nietzsche referred, most of the time, to a particular capacity possessed by one who easily detects values, ranks them instantaneously and, in very rare cases, creates new values himself. Today, such an understanding of instinct may seem rather forced, but Hegel, as well as many authors of his era, evoked an *instinct of reason (Instinkt der Vernunft)* in *The Phenomenology of Spirit* without the fear of being misunderstood.

Like any faculty of the human soul, such as thinking, memory or imagination, *the instinct* for values is more or less developed and, also, it can manifest in a crude form or it can be polished through education. In the absence of appropriate stimuli, the valuating instinct (*Wert-Instinkt*) atrophies to extinction, a process Friedrich Nietzsche called *instinct degeneration (Instinkt-Entartung).*[6] The decadence of modern civilization is ultimately reduced to a degeneration of the instinct for values, as specified in a fragment from *The Twilight of the Idols* entitled *Criticism of Modernity*: "Our institutions are no longer fit for anything: everyone is unanimous about that. But the fault lies not in them but in *us*. Having lost all the instincts out of which institutions grow, we are losing the institutions themselves, because

---

5   Giovanni Papini, *Amurgul filosofilor*, Editura Uranus, Bucureşti, 1991, p. 181.
6   Friedrich Nietzsche, *Twilight of the Idols*, p. 106.

we are no longer fit for them".[7] This is an example of context standing for definition. It is obvious that, in this fragment, the term *instinct* does not in any case have a biological meaning, but an axiological one. Therefore, it is about *Wert-Instinkte*, as specified in the following paragraph: "The *décadence* in the valuating instinct of our politicians, our political parties, goes so deep that *they instinctively prefer* that which leads to dissolution, that which hastens the end".[8]

For Friedrich Nietzsche, the origin of values was synonymous with the origin of man and his history. Human nature is inconceivable without reference to values, no matter how degenerate they may be. The idea that emerges with a certain clarity in Nietzsche's metaphorical discourse is that true values are instincts of the spirit. Concerning "free spirits", or a strong and independent human nature, his instinct for values never failed. But, when it came to the *weak* or the *half-witted*, then values were devalued and the degeneration of man and society would inevitably occur.

2. The hierarchy of values

Values, by their nature, must be categorized. When Friedrich Nietzsche proclaimed, metaphorically, the crushing of the tablets of human values, like paving the way for the establishment of the superman's values, the hierarchy problem of the new values reappeared, with all that this entailed. What is the criterion for hierarchy? Who applies it and who guarantees the accuracy of this application? An objective hierarchy could be created by a philosopher who lies beyond good and evil, but this is just wishful thinking, a requirement, as Friedrich Nietzsche said.[9] He knew very well that this is an absolutely utopian perspective.

Friedrich Nietzsche's solution to the problem of the hierarchy of values was particularly ingenious and deserves full attention from researchers in the fascinating field of values and culture. The "criterion" for the hierarchy of all values, not only moral values, should be *the will to power*. This is not a proper hierarchy criterion, but it acts *as if* it is an axiological standard.

---

7   Ibidem, p. 104.
8   Ibidem, p. 104.
9   Ibidem, p. 66.

We use the phrase *as if* in the sense assigned by Hans Vaihinger in his famous work *Die Philosophie des Als-Ob*. In short, a correct hierarchy of values consists, according to Friedrich Nietzsche, in leaving them free in order to fight each other for survival and for supremacy. The result of this war of everyone against everyone would be a healthy hierarchy of values and, therefore, a strong civilization, lively and free from corruption. Because what else is corruption if not a falsification of a hierarchy of values?

Following such a tough, but fair, confrontation, the *weak* will be removed from the high positions they unjustly occupy and will be put in their place, namely at the bottom of the hierarchy of values. This is a central idea of Friedrich Nietzsche's axiology, but one which has been too little highlighted until now or which has been downright ignored. It is obvious that it was not clearly formulated anywhere, but it is metaphorically expressed both in *Thus Spoke Zarathustra* and in his works during the reconsideration of all values. Anyone who artificially establishes a criterion for the hierarchy of values considers himself to be in possession of truth. In this regard, Friedrich Nietzsche said that "the man is wise as long as he is searching for the truth, but when he thinks that he has found it, he becomes a fool".[10] Denying any criterion alleged to be an objective of a hierarchy of values, he leaves unobstructed the path of permanently seeking for the truth and the fierce fight to acquire it. The idea of this fight for prestige, on the one hand, and, on the other hand, a terminology where a significant share means occupies concepts such as "superman", "will to power", "master-morality", "slave-morality", "instinct" and "degeneration" led to Friedrich Nietzsche being classified as an evolutionist. His conception of values would therefore be an axiological Darwinism. But he vehemently rejected this interpretation, characterizing those who suspected him of Darwinism as "learned cattle".[11]

Modern society is "weak", "degenerate", "decadent" precisely because Christian values have made it ill, by providing undeserved protection to the weak and unfairly and deviously persecuting the strong. As long as *mercy*

---

10 Mazzino Montinari, *Friedrich Nietzsche. Eine Einführung*, Walter de Gruyter, Berlin, 1991, p. 65.

11 Friedrich Nietzsche, *Ecce Homo*, available at https://archive.org/details/The CompleteWorksOfFriedrichNietzschevol.17-EcceHomo. Accessed February 28, 2016.

represents a central value of society, *evil* broke heavily in individual and collective existence. *Value* means "all that heightens the feeling of power, the will to power, power itself in man", while *non-value*, generally expressed by *evil*, means "all that proceeds from weakness".[12] *Mercy* for the weak is harmful because, in this way, evil enters the world. The place of the value system centred on *mercy* must be taken by a system of virtues based on the will to power. "The weak and ill-constituted shall perish: first principle of *our* philanthropy. And one shall help them to do so".[13] This type of discourse was from the beginning regarded with suspicion and still is today. The question often arose as to whether Friedrich Nietzsche was still in his right mind when he wrote *The Antichrist. You shall not have mercy for the weak* seems to be an unacceptable moral principle for any civilization, not only for a Christian one, because anyone can be considered "weak". But Nietzsche's thesis about classifying values *without mercy* is particularly subtle and it is directed against the counterfeits that have been created and are still created under the guise of morality. *Mercy* is the symbol of the *extra-value* criterion of the hierarchy of values. Christianity is only one case among others of the rigging of the axiological order. Even today, it takes a lot of *courage* and *honesty* to say that; however, Friedrich Nietzsche was right: in the context of the hierarchy of value, mercy, as well as any other arbitrary criterion, is disastrous. A fair fight of all values against everyone would lead automatically to a strong spirituality, for the good of everybody, including the *weak* or the *half-witted*.

In any case, when Friedrich Nietzsche said "The weak and ill-constituted shall perish: first principle of *our* philanthropy", he did not mean the *weak* (*schwach*) from a biological, economic or social point of view, but only the weak as bearers of values and creators of values. For instance, someone *weak* in terms of academic training, such as a weak teacher, a weak physician or a weak engineer can cause huge harm to society if they are erroneously or fraudulently placed at the top of the hierarchy of values, each in his field. Who would willingly put himself into a *weak* surgeon's hands and who would travel in a plane flown by a pilot with *weak* training? Such a *weak* man shall perish, Friedrich Nietzsche would say. The *weak*, in the

---

12 Friedrich Nietzsche, *The Antichrist*, Penguin Books, 2003, p. 127.
13 Ibidem, 128.

axiological meaning of the term, must leave the place they do not deserve in the hierarchy of values to be replaced by someone who really does represent high values. Through such tough but fair choices, a vigorous civilization will be established, said Nietzsche. "I formulate a principle. All naturalism in morality, that is all *healthy* morality, is dominated by an instinct of life ... *Anti-natural*, that is virtually every morality that has hitherto been taught, reverenced and preached, turns on the contrary precisely *against* the instincts of life – it is a now secret, now loud and impudent *condemnation* of these instincts".[14]

With regard to the "weak", which must perish, Friedrich Nietzsche provided sufficient explanation showing that he had in mind the axiological sense of the term. In the fragment entitled *Anti-Darwin* in *The Twilight of the Idols*, he said that the famous *struggle for existence* is actually "the fight for power". "Supposing, however, that this struggle exists – and it does indeed occur – its outcome is the reverse of that desired by the school of Darwin, ... namely, the defeat of the stronger, the more privileged, the fortunate exceptions ... Darwin forgot the mind (– that is English!): *the weak possess more mind* ... To acquire mind one must need mind – one loses it when one no longer needs it ... One will see that under mind I include foresight, patience, dissimulation, great self-control, and mimicry".[15] Mercy, as a central value of Christianity, is also a mimetic value.

The criticism that Friedrich Nietzsche brought to Christianity in *The Antichrist* can, in its essence, be generalized and applied to any moral or, more precisely, to any civilization based on a certain moral. For instance, he had read in translation *The Laws of Manu*, in which he found a classic example of religious *pia fraus*.[16] What Nietzsche was interested in, in particular, was the halting of the degeneration of European culture and its revitalization by removal of the "weak" who determined what was good and what was evil. "The problem I raise here is ... what type of human being one ought to *breed*, ought to *will*, as more valuable, more worthy of life, more certain of the future. This more valuable type has existed often enough already:

---

14 Friedrich Nietzsche, *Twilight of the Idols*, p. 55.
15 Ibidem, p. 87.
16 Cf. Mazzino Montinari, op. cit, p. 116.

but ... the reverse type has been willed, bred, the sick animal man".[17] This superior type, which represents "a sort of superman",[18] is the one which would normally be at the top of the hierarchy of values, but Christianity, as well as any other system of morality, "has waged a *war to the death* against this *higher* type of man, ... has depraved the reason even of the intellectually strongest natures by teaching men to feel the supreme values of intellectuality as sinful, as misleading, as *temptations*".[19] Viewed from this perspective, the values that are traditionally considered superior are actually signs of man's and society's degeneration. Friedrich Nietzsche's enunciation of the value of fundamental evaluations in European culture was so clear that it left no room for any interpretation: "my assertion is that all the values in which mankind at present summarizes its highest desideratum are *décadence values*".[20] The solution he proposed is known: *Revaluation of all values!* As a spirit which became free, as he defined himself, he was himself already part of this apocalyptic process of revaluation of all values. His discourse sounds like a sort of *Apocalypse by Nietzsche.*

As is well known, *The Antichrist*, completed in Turin in 1888, was conceived as the first part of a vast paper called *Der Wille zur Macht. Versuch einer Umwertung aller Werte*; however, the title for this in the last plan drawn in September 1888, a title that would probably have remained forever, was *Umwertung aller Werte*. From that moment Friedrich Nietzsche fell into a state of total euphoria. From now on, he no longer knew any measure.[21] The revaluation of all values was his almost obsessive project, a project that led him to fall permanently mentally ill. Further still, even after his madness appeared and his discourse became incoherent, *Umwertung aller Werte* remained noteworthy as the last shining star in the night of his mind.

The problem of value is not central only to the last part of Friedrich Nietzsche's life and work, as often stated in the literature, but, in different forms, it is a constant of his highly poetic philosophy. *Value* and *value*

---

17 Friedrich Nietzsche, *The Antichrist*, p. 128.
18 Ibidem.
19 Ibidem, p. 129.
20 Ibidem.
21 Mazzino Montinari, op. cit., p. 121.

judgements are the only actual philosophical subjects in Friedrich Nietzsche's work and they are ones for which he has a totally remarkable *sense, instinct* and talent.

As for the *revaluation of all values*, it was often noticed that this is not a novelty, that such revaluations are common phenomena in history and are known to scholars. The famous Jacob Burckhardt, from Basel, Nietzsche's friend and colleague for a period of time, had deeply reflected in his own way in the books dedicated to man's radical changes of perspective on values in ancient Greek culture or the Italian Renaissance. But Friedrich Nietzsche raises the problem for the first time to the one who conducts this *Umwertung*. In other words, he raises directly and sometimes brutally the problem of the evaluator's fairness and his always questionable criteria. If the war declared against all values until then ends with the victory of the free spirits in whose name Friedrich Nietzsche speaks, then we all become free spirits; all our creations and acts will finally find the place they deserve in the new hierarchy of values. As in any fairy tale, good would overcome evil, and everyone would live happily ever after and would look to Friedrich Nietzsche as the last saviour.

3. The conflict of values

In Friedrich Nietzsche's conception, there is master-morality and there is slave-morality, indicating that to him *Moral* meant a whole system of values. He stated that these are two types of morality, which all systems of values that can be found in historical reality fall under. Friedrich Nietzsche was undeservedly criticized because, in this respect, he was too schematic and insufficiently documented and he ignored the particularly complex axiological aspects of the various civilizations. But he is only building what Max Weber later called *ideal types*. Friedrich Nietzsche knew very well "that in all higher and mixed civilizations, there are also attempts at the reconciliation of the two moralities, but one finds still oftener the confusion and mutual misunderstanding of them, indeed sometimes their close juxtaposition – even in the same man, within one soul".[22] The end of this

---

22 Friedrich Nietzsche, *Beyond Good and Evil*, available at https://www.gutenberg.org/ebooks/4363. Accessed February 28, 2016.

passage from *Beyond Good and Evil* takes up a well-known idea from Goethe's *Faust*: "*Two souls, alas, are dwelling in my breast, / And one is striving to forsake its brother*".[23]

Only the strong are able to impose moral standards and to establish religious, aesthetic or even scientific values. *Value* is everything that the strong, who have become *masters* due to their power, designate, while all that is associated with the weak, who have become *slaves*, is *non-value*.

In order to properly understand Friedrich Nietzsche, we must say that, this time too, the context stands for definition. Nowhere did he define *master* and *slave*, but any informed reader immediately thinks of the famous chapter *Lordship and Bondage* in Hegel's *Phenomenology of Spirit*. It is about that war to the knife going on between the two self-consciousness to recognize the value of each. Hegel described how the loser is turned into a slave, but the fight continues in subtle forms so that, eventually, the slave becomes the master. He is the chosen one through which universal history takes another step towards the goal set by the good Lord. Friedrich Nietzsche took over from Hegel the idea of the fight for value, but he interpreted its results completely differently. In short, the *strong* are entitled to dominate and to impose their own values, while the *weak* should rightly be *slaves*. This would be the natural axiological order. The deregulation of society or its degeneration or illness occurs when the *weak*, by all kinds of ruses, come to dominate and impose their own system of values.

The strong man, said Friedrich Nietzsche, naturally becomes an *aristocrat* and "regards *himself* as a determiner of values; he does not require to be approved of; he passes the judgment: "What is injurious to me is injurious in itself"; he knows that it is he himself only who confers honour on things; he is a *creator of values*. He honours whatever he recognizes in himself: such morality equals self-glorification".[24] The strong man, an aristocrat in the original meaning of the term, is the measure of all things. It would be wrong to understand that in this way Nietzsche was an apologist for violence and strength of a pagan type. His discourse is axiological, emphasizing the

---

23 Johann Wolfgang Goethe, *Faust*, Editura Univers, Bucureşti, 1982, p. 77.

24 Friedrich Nietzsche, *Beyond Good and Evil*, available at https://www.gutenberg. org/ebooks/4363. Accessed February 28, 2016.

prestige, value, creation of values. The morality of slaves is totally different from the morality of aristocrats. "The slave has an unfavourable eye for the virtues of the powerful; he has a scepticism and distrust, a *refinement* of distrust of everything "good" that is there honoured – he would fain persuade himself that the very happiness there is not genuine ... Slave-morality is essentially the morality of utility".[25] The values of the slave, who fights with the most insidious means to unseat the aristocrat, prove to be a kind of subtle poison and very effective in the long term. Finally, the moral revolt of the slaves will be successful. Society, thus threatened with extinction, being in continuous degeneration, awaits her saviour, none other than Friedrich Nietzsche with his magic formula: *Umwertung aller Werte.*

---

25 Ibidem.

II. The Axioclasm of Friedrich Nietzsche, or Creative Destruction

This essay questions the category of *destroyer* that Friedrich Nietzsche belongs to. He was neither an intellectual terrorist, as he was called, nor an anarchist, as he was also characterized. Despite the fact that nihilism, as a term, became popular through Friedrich Nietzsche's work, he himself was not an nihilist since *Entwertung aller Werte* (devaluation of all values) meant for him only *Entwertung aller christlichen Werte*. His axiology is so unique that it forces us to invent a new term for it: axioclasm.

1. To philosophize with a hammer and sickle

In *The Twilight of the Idols*, and across almost all his work, Friedrich Nietzsche "philosophizes with a hammer", a phenomenon associated, not only by the dilettante reader but also by most commentators, with a certain violence, or interpreted as the gesture of a madman in the psychiatric sense of the term, who, having escaped from the straitjacket, causes havoc around him. Shattering the old values, the favourite subject of Nietzsche's philosophy, takes the form of a set of statues, symbolizing the deepest "truths" of humanity or representing their discoveries, that a madman smashes into pieces. Friedrich Nietzsche's pleasure in destruction was often noted.[26] But this passion for violent destruction had nothing to do with his thinking.

First of all, we must bear in mind that in *Thus Spoke Zarathustra* the "hammer" is the main instrument of philosophizing, but it is associated with the "sickle". Therefore, to be fair to Friedrich Nietzsche, the *sickle* and the *hammer* are symbolic of his way of relating to the old tablet of values, which must be broken, but also to the new one, which must be completed with the values of the *superman*. The sickle and the hammer! Those who have experienced communism probably instinctively refuse the association between these symbols of the torture of the spirit with Friedrich Nietzsche's philosophy, one dedicated par excellence to some free spirits, as mentioned

---

26 Günter Seubold / Patrick Baum (Hgs), *Was mir Nietzsche bedeutet*, DenkMal Verlag, Bonn, 2001, p. 23.

in *Human, All Too Human*. For the defenders of the old values, he meta-phorically used the term *herdsmen* (*herdsmen*), but "they call themselves the good and the righteous ... Behold the good and the righteous! Whom do they hate the most? The one who breaks their tablets of values, the breaker, the lawbreaker: – yet that is the creator. Companions the creator seeks and not corpses, nor herds or believers either. Fellow creators the crea-tor seeks, those who inscribe new values on new tablets".[27] For Friedrich Nietzsche, the sickle was a symbol as important as the hammer, because only destruction paves the way for a new type of creation. "Companions the creator seeks, and fellow harvesters: for all that is with him stands ripe for the harvest. But the hundred sickles are lacking ... Companions the creator seeks, and such as know how to whet their sickles. Destroyers they will be called and despisers of good and evil. But harvesters are they and celebrants too".[28]

For *Umwertung aller Werte*, both the hammer and the sickle are indis-pensable instruments for the philosopher. But this is not about exercising any violent action, but conducting an operation with great sensitivity, which can be achieved only by a truly exceptional spirit. Even if in German it is about one and the same word, *Hammer*, Friedrich Nietzsche referred to the *little hammer* used by the physician to stimulate certain body parts to get certain reactions, the interpretation of which contributes to establishing the patient's diagnosis. This is the type of instrument he referred to when he added *How to Philosophize with a Hammer* as subtitle to the *Twilight of the Idols*. As a true physician of culture, Nietzsche listened with "his evil ear" to the sounds produced by his medical "little hammer" as by a tuning fork when he touched on concepts, values, ideas, famous names, ages and everything related to the "nobility" of man. The tablet of values of humanity became for Nietzsche a kind of out-of-tune piano. Everything sounded off-key! A new *Hammer*, a new chord and new music are needed. *Man*'s values must leave room to make way for those of the *superman*.

"My evil eye", evoked by Nietzsche in the preface to the *Twilight of the Idols*, is the one that told him that all man's *values* sound shallow.

---

27 Friedrich Nietzsche, *Thus Spoke Zarathustra*, Oxford University Press, 2008, p. 21.
28 Ibidem, p. 21.

The sounds obtained with his medical little hammer betray the falsehood, hypocrisy and meanness of all "great men". The *idols* are "touched with the hammer as with a tuning fork".[29] The result of this unusual medical-philosophical research is amazing: the emptier such an idol is, the deeper is men's belief in him. *He that has ears to hear, let him hear!* It is no coincidence that this biblical warning was taken up by Nietzsche whenever it came to philosophizing with the hammer. The physician of the culture who uses such an instrument is a philosopher of the ear, if one may say so.[30] He softly hammers "wisdom" and hears that this word sounds like a base coin; he gently touches the "wise" and rattles his virtues, which he preaches like the small change from the pockets of a dishonest merchant.

In order to not be confused with the nihilist, who is also a destroyer of values and who sometimes acts under the guise of a creator,[31] we will call the destroyer of values an *axioclast*, who is thus consciously paving the way to an alleged new creation. Unfortunately, all tyrants and all dictators have justified their monstrous destruction this way. Both nihilist and axioclast have huge destructive potential, but the sources of their devastating force are totally different. Nihilism does not mean the negation of existing values, much less their reversal or revaluation, but the belief that behind every word designating value there is nothing. *Entwertung aller Werte* (devaluation of all values): this is the definition for nihilism given by Nietzsche. "If a philosopher could be a nihilist, he would be one because he finds nothingness behind all the ideals of man. Or not even nothingness merely – but only the worthless, the absurd, the sick, the cowardly, the weary, dregs of all kinds from the cup of his life *after he has drained it*".[32]

This force of the nihilist is the power of emptiness in a particular cultural atmosphere. As in nature, emptiness gathers around it enormous forces, in the spirit's world, the noting that took the place of values triggers around it devastating forces. Unlike the nihilist, the *axioclast* idolizes only one

---

29 Ibidem.
30 Friedrich Nietzsche, *Aforisme. Scrisori*, Editura Humanitas, Bucureşti, 1992, p. 250.
31 Hermann Rauschning, *Masken und Metamorfosen des Nihilismus*, Humboldt-Verlag, Frankfurt am Main/Wien, 1954, p. 93.
32 Friedrich Nietzsche, *Twilight of the Idols*, p. 96.

value or one class of values, in whose name he destroys all the others. Only through a misunderstanding, which I hope to remove by this distinction, were phenomena like *Bücherverbrennung* or *Entartete Kunst* attributed to some nihilists, whereas they are typical phenomena for what I call *axioclasm*.[33] Iconoclasm is undoubtedly another phenomenon that falls into the broader sphere of axioclasm, just like that which Miguel de Unamuno inspiredly called ideoclasm, which he defined as follows: "There is no tyranny in the world more hateful than that of ideas. Ideas bring ideophobia, and the consequence is that people begin to persecute their neighbours in the name of ideas. I loathe and detest all labels, and the only label that I could now tolerate would be that of *ideoclast* or idea-breaker".[34] Axioclasm has manifested in history as the fanatical destruction of things bearing values, such as books, works of art and monuments and has taken an extreme form in the destruction of their authors. Heinrich Heine's warning referred in fact to the anger of axioclasts: "Wherever they burn books, in the end will human beings also be burned".

When one value is transformed into a simulacrum of a god, on its behalf, the axiologist destroys by worshipping. It is not a coincidence that many such acts of destruction have been carried out ritually.

Nietzsche's *superman* is, in essence, an axioclast. The largest chapter of *Thus Spoke Zarathustra* is for that matter dedicated to shattering the old tablets of values in order to establish new ones. "Here I sit and wait, with old shattered tablets around me as well as new half-inscribed tablets … When I came to human beings I found them sitting on an old conceit: all of them believed they had long known what good and evil were for the human being".[35] The destruction preached by Zarathustra is accompanied by voluptuousness, being carried out grandiosely and accompanied by a genuine ecstasy.

---

33 Nicolae Râmbu, *Two axiological illnesses*, Journal of Human Values, SAGE, vol. 21/2, 2015, pp. 64–71.

34 Miguel de Unamuno, *Ideocraţia*, in vol.: *Eseişti spanioli*, Editura Univers, Bucureşti, 1982, p. 155.

35 Friedrich Nietzsche, *Thus Spoke Zarathustra*, p. 170.

"The human is something that must be overcome".[36] In his style, Nietzsche recognized that this wording of *Thus Spoke Zarathustra* did not belong to him but was like a flower picked on the road, to form the fundamental concept of his philosophy, *overhuman*.[37] Both were taken from Goethe's *Faust*. Because man is a being incapable of moral progress, as demonstrated by Schopenhauer, Friedrich Nietzsche's great master, he must perish and give way to the *overhuman* or *superman*. In *Thus Spoke Zarathustra*, the term commonly used to express more clearly this excellence of man as a stage in the emerging of the *superman* is "*Untergang*", which we find in Oswald Spengler's famous book *Der Untergang des Abendlandes*. Zarathustra's axioclasm reaches its peak precisely in the fascination for this apocalyptic *Untergang*. "I love those who would not preserve themselves. Those who go under I love with my entire love: for they also go over".[38] This impulse towards destruction, which can easily be noticed in all Friedrich Nietzsche's writing, was interpreted as a sign of his native madness.[39]

"O my brothers, shatter, shatter for me the old tablets".[40] This exhortation, repeated numerous times by Zarathustra, expresses the essence of axioclasm. What should the new tablet of values, in whose name all this *Untergang* is taking place, look like? Nietzsche's answer to this question was essentially this: "there is need of a *new nobility* that is the opponent of all rabble and everything despotic and writes anew on new tablets the word "noble"".[41] What did Friedrich Nietzsche reproach in the old system of value? The fact that these belong to the "weak" people, who always resort to intrigue, calumny and hypocrisy to prevent the "strong" occupying the place they would deserve in an authentic hierarchy. "Verily, not to a nobility that you could buy like shopkeepers and with shopkeepers" gold: for of little value is anything that has its price".[42] The daises of virtue, like all places from which human and superhuman values are preached, must be

---

36 Ibidem, p. 171.
37 Ibidem.
38 Ibidem, p. 173.
39 Gisela Deesz, *Die Entwicklung des Nietzsche-Bildes in Deutschland*, Würzburg, 1933, p. 47.
40 Friedrich Nietzsche, *Thus Spoke Zarathustra*, p. 175.
41 Ibidem, p. 176.
42 Ibidem.

destroyed in order to build on their ruins a mountain, from the top of which the values of the *superman* could be announced. The so-called good and righteous, according to the old axiological formation, hate the real creator the most. "They crucify him who writes new values on new tablets ... With whom does the greatest danger for all human future lie? Is it not the good and the righteous? *Shatter, shatter for me the good and the righteous! ...* False coasts and false securities the good taught you. Everything has been lied about and twisted around down to its ground by the good".[43]

Zarathustra is the embodiment of axioclasm because he preaches with all clarity the destruction of human values as a first step towards establishing the superman's values. Friedrich Nietzsche did not define anywhere the concept of the *Übermensch*, and he made no reference to its numerous uses in Christian theology and mysticism.[44] He also made no reference to any author who uses this term, not even Goethe, from whom he took, without doubt, not only the word as such, but also certain formulas linked to *superman*.

In *Ecce Homo*, Friedrich Nietzsche drew attention to the fact that the term *Übermensch* would be much misunderstood. At least three false meanings of the *superman*, to which he expressly drew attention in the chapter *Why I Write Such Good Books*, were to be avoided. *Firstly*, he should not be conceived of as the "*idealistic* type or as a superior man, half saint, half genius".[45] *Übermensch* is not therefore an ideal towards which man should strive and which he may reach sometime, in a distant future, but a completely different kind of existence. The superman is essentially the non-man.

Secondly, the superman must not be understood in the light of Darwinism as an overvalued man. The entire discourse of Nietzsche's *On the Superior Human* is ironic, in the sense that this is always a counterfeit.

The man, "the little god of the world", as characterized by Goethe in Faust, "is as whimsical as on Creation's day", which means that, in his essence, he remained unchanged and he will never change, despite all the efforts

---

43 Ibidem, p. 186.

44 Ernst Benz, *Der Übermensch*, Rhein-Verlag, Zürich/Stuttgart, 1961, p. 65.

45 Friedrich Nietzsche, *Ecce Homo*, available at https://archive.org/details/The CompleteWorksOfFriedrichNietzschevol.17-EcceHomo. Accessed February 28, 2016.

of the "humanity improvers". This is the sad truth about the "little god" that Goethe expressed through Mephistopheles: the man "could have lived a little bit better / If you wouldn't have gave him your heavenly spark. / He says it's reason [*Vernunft*], but through it / Neither the beast is more evil than him".

By *Übermensch*, Friedrich Nietzsche was only expressing in a more philosophical manner Goethe's idea of man as an animal sick in by *Vernunft* or *Geist*. All values of man that are represented by this *Geist* are actually symptoms of the sickness of his essence. "The man who unmasks morality has also unmasked the worthlessness of the values in which men either believe or have believed; he no longer sees anything to be revered in the most venerable man – even in the types of men that have been pronounced holy; all he can see in them is the most fatal kind of abortions, fatal because they fascinate".[46] The spirit of man, said Nietzsche, is a moral vampire, because it consumes the lifeblood. Life is serving the spirit, the other way round. The *superman*, through a certain violence, breaks forever this axiological order, where the man is mutilated to match his "values" and puts life ahead of spirit. When Spirit (*Geist*) appears at Faust's call, he says: "Terrible to see!"[47] In this context, Faust is, ironically, called *superman*, in the sense of a human who is more inclined than any other to put his life completely in the service of spirit. Friedrich Nietzsche took the term *Übermensch* from Goethe, but he tacitly attached to it a totally opposite meaning. The superman preached by Zarathustra has as a principle "Pereat veritas, fiat vita".[48]

The world of human values, like pearls, is the result of an illness.[49] This is why Friedrich Nietzsche, through the characters in his philosophical poem *Thus Spoke Zarathustra*, blew up the old tablet of values and proudly said "*Ich bin kein Mensch, ich bin Dynamit*".[50]

Thirdly, the superman is not the hero, in the sense Carlyle ascribed to this term.

---

46 Ibidem.
47 Johann Wolfgang Goethe, *Faust*, available at https://www.gutenberg.org/files/14591/14591-h/14591-h.htm#I. Accessed February 28, 2016.
48 Theodor Lessing, *Nietzsche*, Ullstein Verlag, Berlin, 1925, p. 61.
49 Ibidem, p. 61.
50 Friedrich Nietzsche, *Ecce Homo*, in: Gesammelte Werke, Gondrom Verlag, Bindlach, 2005, p. 1231.

Friedrich Nietzsche's conception of *superman* is not another conception of the *new man*, but a reply given to those who believed that man himself can be transfigured. In other words, a true change in the face of man has never happened and it is not possible in the future. The *new man* of Christianity is nothing more than a caricature of the old man. The result of all religious and political movements to create a new man was *Human, All Too Human*. All old imperfections of man were masked in the most treacherous manner by Christianity. Friedrich Nietzsche, who was for a long time a disciple of Schopenhauer, knows that human nature, fundamentally evil, can never be changed. So what should be done, then? Man is something that must be overcome, Nietzsche raved and stormed, repeating this statement from *Faust*.

2. The machine that produces glory

Through a serious misunderstanding or perhaps through an abusive interpretation, Friedrich Nietzsche has often been categorized among dangerous thinkers, "who, in the place of love and devotion, they put hatred and selfishness, in the place of the beautiful and sublime, the ugly and what is common, in the place of truth, the lie, in the place of peaceful relations and community of interests, the general war, in short, in all areas, in the place of order, the wildest anarchy, non-order and complete illegality".[51] Friedrich Nietzsche was "reached in high esteem among those who support anarchy in any field, even in the art".[52] The slogan of the Oriental sect of Assassins, said Hermann Türck, became the only moral principle recognized by Nietzsche: "Nothing is true, everything is permitted".[53] Indeed, the *Shadow* chapter from *Thus Spoke Zarathustra* seems to be a rewriting of the story of Marco Polo about the *Old Man in the Mountains and His Hashashins*. Intoxicated with hashish and promised heaven, the *hashashins* blindly listened to the old man and killed at his command.

But Friedrich Nietzsche, far from being a modern follower of the Assassin sect, was a subtle critic of them and especially of all forms of criminal

---

51 Hermann Türck, *Omul genial*, Editura Socec, Bucureşti, 1898, p. 37.
52 Ibidem.
53 Ibidem.

fanaticism resulting in what Ceslaw Milosz later called *captive thinking*. Political or religious ideologies proceed like the old man in the mountains who promises the young men supreme happiness: he "drugs" them with a few "truths" produced by skilled and crafty artisans, as Cassirer called the inventors of the political myths of the twentieth century, and sends them to kill. The *Shadow* chapter from Zarathustra expresses precisely the need to shatter these prefabricated "truths" acting in the same way the drug acted on the *hashashins*: "With you I shattered whatever my heart had revered; all boundary-stones and images I overthrew; ... With you I unlearned my belief in words and values and great names ... "Nothing is true, everything is permitted": thus I spoke to myself ... Ah, where has all my goodness gone, and all shame and all belief in those who are good! Ah, where is that mendacious innocence that I once possessed, the innocence of the good and their noble lies!".[54]

What would be Nietzsche's solution to morality based on the principle "Nothing is true, everything is permitted"? Anarchy! This is the moral solution when *God has died*. Today, in general, *anarchy* is a derogatory term, but for Nietzsche, a philologist sensitive to subtle etymologies, the term made reference first of all to the Greek *an-arche*. It is about the lack of a unique principle of hierarchy of values, whose symbol was for centuries God. *An-arche* is the natural consequence of the death of God. Despite the concern of the *good* and *righteous*, the idealists and *believers* of any kind, the *anarchy of values*, announced by Friedrich Nietzsche, as remarked by Paul Valadier, also has a number of positive effects. "The anarchy of values does not mean lack of values, shapeless chaos and disappearance of all principles of thinking and life. We must say that precisely the opposite is true".[55] A unit of values that revolves around God is a utopia, an ideal that has nothing to do with reality. There were always more systems of values, and the multicivilizational nature of our world is an undeniable reality.

In an excerpt from *The Gay Science* called *Why We Are Not Idealists*, Friedrich Nietzsche expressed with all clarity the fact that the *idealist* is more likely to be dangerous than elative for the human spirit. He protested

---

54 Friedrich Nietzsche, *Thus Spoke Zarathustra*, pp. 238–239.
55 Paul Valadier, *L'anarchie des valeurs*, in: "Cultura: International Journal of Philosophy of Culture and Axiology", 3/1, 2006, p. 89–100.

vehemently whenever he was referred to as an idealist and stated that every page he wrote was a sign of the fierce fight that he took up against idealism. When Friedrich Nietzsche, through Zarathustra, said that the *idea* of God was the greatest danger for mankind, he did nothing other than express metaphorically the thesis according to which the *anarchy of values* is preferable to the tyranny of the unique principle, being more in line with real life and the true needs of humanity.

A French author contemporary with Nietzsche, Villiers de l'Isle-Adam, wrote an interesting story called *La Machine à Gloire*. In short, it is about an extraordinary invention, a machine that produces glory. From what? From anything. Friedrich Nietzsche's entire axioclasm is directed towards such a *Machine à Gloire*. The state, like the church, is the model of such a machine. "All things it will give *you*, if you worship it, the new idol: thus it buys itself the lustre of your virtue and the glance of your proud eyes".[56] The state, this infernal machine, transforms men into madmen. "Madmen they all seem to me, and clambering apes and overardent".[57] The exhortation of Zarathustra to the superior people is to destroy the state, along with all similar machines, like the church: "There where the state *ceases* – cast your glance over there, my brothers! Do you not see it, the rainbow and the bridges of the Overhuman?".[58]

The machine of glory, which makes virtues from vices, "geniuses" from the "flies of the public market", a model of wisdom from the opportunist without scruples, was described by Friedrich Nietzsche in almost the same terms as Villiers de l'Isle-Adam: "In this world even the finest things amount to nothing without someone to make a show of them: great men the people call these showmen. Little do the people comprehend what is great – that is, the creative. But they do have a sense for all showmen and play-actors of great matters. Around inventors of new values the world revolves – invisibly it revolves. Yet around play-actors the people and fame revolve: that is "the way of the world"".[59] In the hands of an opportunist, the machine of glory produces the "values" needed to manipulate others and make them

---

56 Friedrich Nietzsche, *Thus Spoke Zarathustra*, p. 44.
57 Ibidem.
58 Ibidem, p. 45.
59 Ibidem, p. 45.

believe in him. In today's terms, it might be said that the truth is a matter of show. The content of a statement means nothing: putting it in the scene is everything. The "arranger" of *Thus Spoke Zarathustra*: "tomorrow has a new belief and the day after tomorrow a newer one ... To bowl over – that he calls: to demonstrate. To drive frantic – that he calls: to convince. And blood counts for him as the best of all grounds".[60] Friedrich Nietzsche knew all about *statute labour*, that group of people who, at the theatre or opera, were paid to applaud or boo. The phenomenon is described in the *Memoirs of an Idealistic Woman*,[61] a book he considered "very uncommon", as one can read in Nietzsche's letter to Carl Fuchs, dated July 1877.[62]

The superman is the alternative to "man", who operates the machine of glory. He is also the axioclast who, ultimately, no longer focuses on the revaluation of all values, but, based on this, on a type of creation completely new, completely unknown and also inaccessible to "man". Zarathustra, the messenger of superman, knows that in front of these "solemn jesters" there is no chance of completely destroying false values, because they will produce others, but the machine that produces glory must be destroyed. The *arrangers*, handlers of this infernal machine, "are skilful, with clever fingers: what does *my* simplicity want with their multiplicity! All kinds of threading and knotting and weaving their fingers understand: thus they work at the stockings of the spirit ... Inventive in petty craftiness, they wait for those whose knowing walks on lame feet – like spiders they wait. I have seen them always carefully preparing their poisons; and they always put on gloves of glass beforehand. They also know how to play with loaded dice; and I have found them playing so eagerly that they were sweating".[63]

Although *Thus Spoke Zarathustra* is a poem and it should be treated as such, there are several passages where Friedrich Nietzsche indicated very clearly how *superman* should be understood, by emphasizing the prefix

---

60 Ibidem, pp. 45–46.
61 Malwida von Meysenbug, *Memorien einer Idealistin*, Zweiter Band, Schuster & Loeffler Verlag, Berlin und Leipzig, 1899, pp. 287–293.
62 Friedrich Nietzsche, *Aforisme. Scrisori*, Editura Humanitas, Bucureşti, 1992, p. 212.
63 Friedrich Nietzsche, *Thus Spoke Zarathustra*, p. 109.

super (*über*). For instance, in the chapter *About Scholars*, *über* has the meaning of *above* or *over* what the machine of glory produces as "scholars" (*Gelehrten*). About these, Zarathustra said "We are alien to each other, and their virtues go even more against my taste than their falsehoods and loaded dice. And when I lived among them, I lived above them. *Over* that they became angry at me ... But notwithstanding I pass with my thoughts *over* their heads; and even if I wanted to walk on my own mistakes, I would still be above them and over their heads. For human beings are *not* equal: thus speaks justice. And what I want, *they* would have no right to want".[64]

The machine of glory, typical to the *man* produced and produces "nobility" upon request and against remuneration, as any good; this is why, Nietzsche said, through Zarathustra, nobility should be redefined, and all values should be revaluated and rearranged honestly in a new hierarchy. In axiology, in the foundation of which Friedrich Nietzsche's work played a crucial role, the distinction is made between things that are valuable and can be sold and those that only have value that cannot be measured in money. Unfortunately, man has become the measure of all things in the sense that he reduces everything, ultimately, to what is measurable by money. The first time a person was measured with another person was in the relation between seller and buyer, said Friedrich Nietzsche. "No level of civilization, however rudimentary, has been found where something of this relationship cannot be discerned. Setting prices, estimating values, devising equivalents, making exchanges ... this all arrives at the great generalization: "Everything has its price, *everything* can be paid off" ".[65]

The old tablet of values which Friedrich Nietzsche was criticizing was, in fact, a price list. This idea was expressed with complete clarity by Nicolas Fouquet, finance minister of Ludovic XIV: "I have all the money of the Kingdom and I know the price of every virtue!" The machine that produces glory is not merely the literary fiction of a "degenerate", but a reality that the "wise" are pretending not to see, although it is precisely they who handle it in the shadows. This is what Friedrich Nietzsche wanted, with his *superman*: a world in which the merchants of glory and nobility become insolvent. If man, by his nature, is incapable of reforming himself from a moral point of

64 Ibidem, p. 109.
65 Friedrich Nietzsche, *On the Genealogy of Morals*, pp. 51–52.

view, he must be helped to perish. "The most concerned minds today ask: "How is the human to be preserved?" But Zarathustra is the first and only one to ask: "How is the human to be *overcome*?"".[66]

This idea of the human *overcome* is not new. And I am not referring only to the fact that Friedrich Nietzsche took from Goethe's *Faust* the formula "the human is something that must be overcome", but also to all conceptions that have advocated the idea of the *new human*. The *superman* metaphorically expresses the sad truth that a *change in the face* of the human is impossible.

The risk of the anarchy of values, which occurs after "the old God has died",[67] is not underestimated by Friedrich Nietzsche; on the contrary, he drew attention to the fact that, metaphorically speaking, a place that remains empty can be occupied by the devil. This is actually the warning sent in *The Ass Festival*: if God has died, then anyone and anything can be deified, even a ass.

3. The sadism of Friedrich Nietzsche

Friedrich Nietzsche's destructive impulse, extensive enough that he considered himself, metaphorically speaking, more dynamite than man, was interpreted, among others, as a sign of his sadism. This is Max Nordau's point of view in his work *Entartung*, the title of which is a term commonly used by Nietzsche as a synonym for decadence. "There are few pains so grievous as to have seen, divined, or experienced how an exceptional man has missed his way and deteriorated (*entartete*)".[68] Moreover, man himself has degenerated and this general degeneration of man produced the deepest anguish in Nietzsche, because it results in a society of men who are equal, without personality, as if they were mass-manufactured products.

From Friedrich Nietzsche's perspective, modern man appears as follows: a sick man, degenerate, like the whole of modern civilization. But, from another perspective, Nietzsche himself is a degenerate. By an ironic paradox, in Max Nordau's *Entartung*, published when he was still alive but severely

---

66 Friedrich Nietzsche, *Thus Spoke Zarathustra*, p. 250.
67 Ibidem, p. 260.
68 Friedrich Nietzsche, *Beyond Good and Evil*, available at https://www.gutenberg.org/ebooks/4363. Accessed February 28, 2016.

mentally ill, Nietzsche's philosophy is presented as a *degenerate* philosophy. Such a creation, said Max Nordau, is the symptom of a degenerate author – Friedrich Nietzsche's entire body of work was proof of the fact that he suffered from egotism. When you read with a certain axiological neutrality any of his work, claimed Nordeau, you feel like you are dealing with a furious madman who talks excessively, sometimes exclusively about himself, and who wants at all costs to impose the few fixed ideas that are obsessing him. Friedrich Nietzsche did not demonstrate or argue for anything, but he dictatorially proclaimed an alleged truth. In doing so, it is no wonder that he constantly contradicted himself, sometimes on the same page. Like any madman, said Max Nordau, he also had some lucid moments: he realized that he contradicted himself and then he claimed that he wanted to have fun by tricking the reader.

A lot of phrases in *Thus Spoke Zarathustra* say nothing; they are simply sequences of words by a madman. Also, all of Friedrich Nietzsche's other works, even those that have seductive titles, are inconsistent, and their lack of content cannot be compensated for with an aphoristic style. When an idea is stated with some clarity, it turns out to be a banality expressed in a form that Nietzsche hoped would amaze.

For instance, *Umwertung aller Werte* was already a commonplace for the theorists of civilizations when Nietzsche presented the *revaluation of all values* as his own epochal breakthrough. Friedrich Nietzsche was original, Max Nordau claimed, only when he was delirious, when his words, although they sounded good, did not have any precise meaning and no longer presented elements of a rational discourse.

The philosophy of the will to power is actually styled after Arthur Schopenhauer, whom Nietzche often referenced as his great master. The *Genealogy of Morals* is addressed to him as a contemporary, as Nietzsche said, with all its passion and with "its secret refutation".[69] But it is precisely in this *refutation* that there lies the secret of the "originality" of Friedrich Nietzsche, who was only reversing in an infantile way a rational discourse. His philosophy was born from the mania of denying, contradicting and arguing with anyone on any topic.

---

69 Friedrich Nietzsche, *On the Genealogy of Morals*, p. 7.

Max Nordau, like Hermann Türck, noticed the fact that, with Friedrich Nietzsche, there is a horrifying association between the representations of various forms of cruelty with a deep sense of pleasure. The diagnosis given by Max Nordau in this case is unforgiving: *sadism*, but this is strictly manifested only spiritually. Indeed, in the *Genealogy of Morals* all references to cruelty are accompanied by the expression of a feeling of satisfaction: "There is no mistaking the predator beneath the surface of all these noble races, the magnificent *blond beast* roaming lecherously in search of booty and victory".[70] The aristocratic races were like predators, whom Nietzsche characterized by "their horrific serenity and deep pleasure in all destruction, in the sensuality of victory and cruelty".[71] The disgust for man, about which he spoke in the *Genealogy of Morals*, comes from the fact that "we no longer have anything to fear from man".[72] *The Gay Science* contains even more fragments illustrating Max Nordau's thesis that we are dealing with a sadistic author in the highest degree. Moreover, the *science* is *cheerful* to the extent that it is "the *great giver of pain*! – And then its counterforce might at the same time be found: its immense capacity for letting new galaxies of joy flare up!".[73] Friedrich Nietzsche outlined "refined cruelty as virtue", a real philosophy of cruelty's producing satisfaction. Talking about "the enjoyment of cruelty" or supporting a thesis that "Cruelty is one of the most ancient enjoyments at their festivities"[74] means expressing oneself like a sadist.

Max Nordau's conclusion about Friedrich Nietzsche's mental health is radical: it concerns an author who was mad even from birth and whose entire body of work is proof of this. Nietzsche's philosophy is, said Max Nordau, an *entartete Philosophie*, produced by a lunatic. In 1892–1893, when the two volumes of the work *Entartung* were published, Friedrich Nietzsche was confined to an asylum, having been committed to it as incurably insane. The question has often been put of how to delimit precisely the texts written when he was profoundly affected by his incurable mental

---

70 Ibidem, p. 26.
71 Ibidem.
72 Ibidem, p. 27.
73 Friedrich Nietzsche, *The Gay Science*, p. 38.
74 Friedrich Nietzsche, *The Dawn of Day*, available at http://www.gutenberg.org/files/39955/39955-h/39955-h.html. Accessed February 28, 2016.

illness. In this respect, Max Nordau was categorical: "He is obviously insane from birth, and his books bear on every page the imprint of insanity. It may be cruel to insist on this fact. It is, however, a painful, yet unavoidable, duty to refer to it anew, because Nietzsche has become the means of raising a mental pestilence, and the only hope of checking its propagation lies in placing Nietzsche's insanity in the clearest light, and in branding his disciples also with the marks most suited to them, viz., as hysterical and imbecile."[75]

At the end of the nineteenth century, it seemed that the whole world had gone mad, being attracted in a magical way by the works of Friedrich Nietzsche, of symbolists and other "degenerates". Their success meant only that civilization itself was in decline. The admirers of Nietzsche can only be personalities similar to their idol: degenerate, sadistic, moronic, hysterical, insane and egotistical.

Nietzsche's madness before his hospitalization, said Max Nordau, consisted of a complex of manias, which resulted in a stranger manner of writing, in which the findings had no relation to the premises, and which was about those few ideas that the author repeated deliriously. If it is true that "the style is the man himself", as Buffon said, then Friedrich Nietzsche's style says everything about the author. In this case, it is mistaken to say that Nietzsche's is an aphoristic style. With rare exceptions, Friedrich Nietzsche was not an author of aphorisms in the strict sense of the word. Also, the fragment representing the essence of the romantic style is not an approach that he would have chosen consciously. His mental illnesses never allowed him, said Max Nordau, to coherently write more than a few pages.

This "Nietzschean" analysis that Max Nordau made of Nietzsche himself falls into the long series of works devoted to the influence of the philosopher's illnesses on his work. The problem that interests us here is how Nietzsche related to values, which are the central subject of his philosophical reflections. Is he a theorist of values? Obviously not, since he merely described in a captivating way, and from a literary point of view, various aspects of the phenomenon of value. Is Friedrich Nietzsche a nihilist? Definitely not, since *Entwertung aller Werte* (devaluation of all values) meant for him only *Entwertung aller christlichen Werte*. Is he an idealist? This time the answer is

---

75 Max Nordau, *Degeneration*, available at https://www.gutenberg.org/files/51161/51161-h/51161-h.htm#c415. Accessed February 12, 2016.

also definitely negative. In a letter to Malwida von Meysenbug, on 20 October 1888, Friedrich Nietzsche reproached her that she had never understood what type of thinker he was, although he sent her all his books. "I have gradually stopped almost all my human relations because of abhorrence as I was treated as someone other than I really am. Now, it is your turn. [...] Because you are "idealistic" ... while any phrase from my writings contains a condemnation [*Verachtung*] of idealism".[76] It can equally be said about Friedrich Nietzsche that he is not a representative of axiological empiricism or any other school of known thought. His axiology is so particular that it forces us to invent a new term to designate it: axioclasm. The destruction of existing values as a prerequisite for a completely new type of creation was expressed by Friedrich Nietzsche as follows: the greatest evil belongs to the greatest good.

---

76 Apud Mario Leis, *Frauen um Nietzsche*, Rowolt Verlag, Hamburg, 2000, p. 62.

III. Friedrich Nietzsche: The Man of Resentment

1. *The reversal of the evaluating gaze*

The biography of a philosopher should not matter too much when it comes to understanding his concepts, ideas or theories. Immanuel Kant's *Critique of Pure Reason*, Leibniz's *Theodicy* or Spinoza's *Ethics* can be understood without turning to the lives of their authors. But Friedrich Nietzsche's ideas have no meaning without reference to the author's life. His philosophy is incomprehensible without biography. And I refer not just to the fact that the further a work is from the system, the more interpretable it is through the life experiences of the author, but also to those few concepts and ideas clearly formulated by Friedrich Nietzsche. To understand his work, you have to know his life and personality very well because Nietzsche wrote only about himself. Let us now take a first example, chosen almost randomly from his work *Human, All Too Human*: "You seek to make the people you cannot stand suspects for you".[77] As everybody knows, there are countless fragments of such an evidently confessional nature in Friedrich Nietzsche's work. Unlike other authors, who use the confessional style of their philosophy mainly to hide behind, rather than to really expose themselves to the prying eyes of the other, the author of *Thus Spoke Zarathustra* was honest, as far as possible, because in every man's conscience there is a certain unconscious or, at best, semi-conscious self-censorship.

Regarding *resentment*, Friedrich Nietzsche was undoubtedly an expert, a significant psychologist and a discoverer of the mechanism of creation of resentment. But *resentment*, as shown by the French term itself, for which he did not find an equivalent in German, is a *sentiment,* and therefore a complex experiment that cannot be theorized, but only described from personal experience. The whole philosophy of resentment that Friedrich Nietzsche exposed, not only in the *Genealogy of Morals* but also in most of his works, is based on his own experience. He made the people he could

---

77 Friedrich Nietzsche, *Omenesc, prea omenesc*, I, in *Opere complete*, vol. 3, Editura Hestia, Timişoara, 2000, p. 224.

not stand *suspects*, as he expressed it in the above-mentioned fragment of *Human, All Too Human*. But who are these? All those in front of whom, in one way or another, he felt inferior. He is the "*weak*" person against whom his relentless criticism is directed to. In short, Friedrich Nietzsche was the *man of resentment* in the highest degree; this is why he madly suspected all the great men of immorality. His place at the top of the hierarchy of values was obtained by fraud. Goethe said that in the face of the superiority of another there is no other means of salvation than love. Friedrich Nietzsche's reaction to the real or imaginary superiority of others is a hidden one, as it is manifested in a soul overwhelmed by resentment.

Let us now describe more precisely the man of resentment, by appealing to Max Scheler. He showed that "first of all, ressentiment is the repeated experiencing and reliving of a particular emotional response reaction against someone else. The continual reliving of the emotion sinks it more deeply into the center of the personality, but concomitantly removes it from the person's zone of action and expression. It is not a mere intellectual recollection of the emotion and of the events to which it "responded" – it is a re-experiencing of the emotion itself, a renewal of the original feeling".[78]

The thesis of this essay is a radical one: Friedrich Nietzsche was hardly a theorist of resentment, as Max Scheler said, but he himself was an embodiment of the man of resentment; he himself was the "slave" always critical of the "master", whose place he would like to take. "The slave revolt in morals begins when *ressentiment* itself becomes creative and ordains values: the *ressentiment* of creatures to whom the real reaction, that of the deed, is denied and who find compensation in an imaginary revenge. While all noble morality grows from a triumphant affirmation of itself, slave morality from the outset says no to "outside", to an "other", to a "non-self": and *this* no is its creative act".[79] Despite some vague references to history, there is no doubt that Friedrich Nietzsche spoke from his own experience in this passage and others like it about *ressentiment*. The reversal of all values becomes the most heartbreaking obsession of the man of resentment,

78 Max Scheler, *Omul resentimentului*, Editura Humanitas, Bucureşti, 2007, pp. 9–10.
79 Friedrich Nietzsche, *On the Genealogy of Morals*, p. 22.

because he himself feels unfairly that he is placed on a lower level of the hierarchy of values.

Despite the errors he made from a historical point of view when referring to "slave-morality", Nietzsche described perfectly from the psychological point of view the type of man who shares such morality. He knew better than anyone else what it means to be penetrated by an unspoken hatred towards those "masters" who are unworthy of determining what is good and what is bad. He also described perfectly, from his own experience, how to be the creator of the man of resentment. Any creation from resentment is based on a negation and ends in a reversal of values. In the *Preface* to the *Genealogy of Morals*, Friedrich Nietzsche said directly that his manner of philosophizing is a bellicose one and it is based on the tendency of saying *no*, of reversing all that is recognized as "value". Of Paul Rée's book *The Origin of Moral Sentiments*, he said "It is possible that I have never read anything which I have rejected so thoroughly, proposition by proposition, conclusion by conclusion, as this book".[80]

For the man of resentment, negation is a sign of some superiority that he is afraid to admit. The man of resentment, when he becomes a creator of culture, is passionate about the object of his negation. This passion that always accompanies the "secret opposition", evoked by Nietzsche, is present in almost every page he wrote. As a man of resentment, as described in the *Genealogy of Morals*, Nietzsche himself suffered from that "*reversal of the evaluating gaze*"[81] in the light of which all values become suspicious. Unlike the "noble", whose nobility always comes from their force, the man of resentment is duplicitous, dishonest, always seeking to betray and planning the most dubious conspiracies. He is completely devoid of nobility.

Friedrich Nietzsche's obsession for nobility, which extended to fancifully rebuilding genealogy in order present himself as royalty, is actually a typical reaction of the "weak", whose morality he combated with a vehemence close to morbidness. "For the *ressentiment* of the noble man himself, if it appears at all, completes and exhausts itself in an immediate reaction. For that reason, it does not *poison*. On the other hand, *ressentiment* simply fails to appear in countless cases where its emergence would be inevitable

---

80 Friedrich Nietzsche, *On the Genealogy of Morals*, p. 7.
81 Ibidem, p. 22.

among the weak and the powerless. To be incapable of taking one's enemies, accidents, even one's *misdeeds* seriously for long – such is the sign of strong full natures".[82] However, the man of resentment, by that "*reversal of the evaluating gaze*", never forgets the "enemy", whom he conceives of as "the evil one", in opposition to himself as "the good one".[83] There is no need to be a skilled psychologist or a well-versed psychoanalyst to realize that, this time also, Friedrich Nietzsche was speaking about himself. His entire body of work is proof that he was overwhelmed by resentment.

Suspecting every creator of values of fraud, Nietzsche made his escape to the insalubrious place where ideals are manufactured.[84] His remarks on this occasion provide the man of resentment with supreme satisfaction: first of all, *merit* is only weakness, then, the inability to exact revenge becomes *kindness*, cowardice magically transforms into *patience*, or, in short, all *values* turn out to be *non-values*. Starting from his life experience, Friedrich Nietzsche discovered in Paul the Apostle and the "new man" of Christianity propagated by him a very special sense of power: the power of those who are powerless or, in other words, the power of the *weak*. In the face of these, there is no way of salvation for the genius besides loneliness, that inhuman loneliness that the philosopher himself lived fully after he left the University of Basel. In the chapter *On the Flies of the Market-Place* in *Thus Spoke Zarathustra*, the author turned to himself when he said "Flee into your solitude! You have lived too close to the petty and the wretched. Flee from their invisible revenge! Toward you they are nothing but revenge … Innumerable are these petty and the wretched creatures; and for the collapse of many a proud structure raindrops and weeds have been sufficient. You are no stone, but you have already become hollow from many drops. You will yet break and burst apart from many drops".[85] If Friedrich Nietzsche had been a noble man, according to the meaning he attributed to this term, then his *resentment* would have instantaneously resolved itself and the "enemy" would have been be forgotten. But *resentment* always returned to his soul, more and more obsessively, more and more intensely and more

---

82 Ibidem, p. 24.
83 Ibidem, p. 22.
84 Ibidem, p. 31.
85 Friedrich Nietzsche, *Thus Spoke Zarathustra*, p. 46.

dangerously for himself, because then, except for a very small group of friends, no one knew about Friedrich Nietzsche and his resentful writings.

2. The philosophy of a loser

Because these days Friedrich Nietzsche is such a famous philosopher, talking about him as a loser may seem a bit exaggerated. But there are many well-documented works about his life and work which show very clearly that we are dealing with a man who failed in all areas: his military career ended miserably when he simply fell off a horse; as a composer, no one has ever taken him seriously; the philosopher's romantic and matrimonial failures are well known today; he did not cut a brilliant figure as a professor at the University of Basel – on the contrary, very few students showed real interest in his classes, so Nietzsche's early retirement was a relief to the academic community; as a philosopher, no one would take any notice of him, no matter how "dangerous" he endeavoured to look; and all his friends gradually left him, eventually leaving him absolutely alone. All these failures, in addition to others that we cannot list here, affected him so deeply that he himself became the man of resentment *par excellence*.

His hidden hatred towards those who managed to reach, both in life and in society, and in culture, the top of the hierarchy of values, was so deep that he exceeded even his own capacity for self-censorship in *The Antichrist*. His virulent reaction against Paul and the Christianity he founded was in fact directed against the world in which Friedrich Nietzsche failed. Like his great master, Arthur Schopenhauer, who had also failed on all levels, Nietzsche interpreted this failure as a sign of nobility: only little people could succeed in "the worst of all possible worlds", as Schopenhauer characterized the world allegedly created by the infinitely good God. The almost morbid need of glory and recognition of his own values can easily be seen in every page written by Friedrich Nietzsche.

In *The Genealogy of Morals* he expressed his belief that no great man would pass the exam of a *real* biography! Lord Byron, Thomas Moore, Schopenhauer, Beethoven are just a few examples Friedrich Nietzsche presented to support the assertion that the entire gallery of great men is counterfeit. In other words, truly great men do not exist; there are only some fake biographies. The lives of saints represent the model of such a forged biography. For this reason, Friedrich Nietzsche frequently stated openly that he was against idealism.

Regarding the biographies gilded with idealism, he was smart enough to write about himself as if he wrote about others. He said that an *Umwertung aller Werte* should be quickly produced so that the *weak*, the men of resentment, who were fraudulently transformed into "great men", would be brought back to the lowest level of the hierarchy of values. None other than Friedrich Nietzsche should occupy the throne atop this hierarchy of values.

As a psychological type, he is a very special case in the history of European culture because the source of his devastating *resentment* is the resentment itself embodied by the "weak", who, through a herd instinct, grouped around the "good shepherd" and took power. They have dominated the world for two millennia, they decide what is good and what is bad, and they arbitrarily share rewards and punishments. In *The Antichrist*, Paul the Apostle is the type of successful man who has used absolutely any means to achieve his goal. Such a human, all too human, type is at the root of Friedrich Nietzsche's resentment. "It is necessary to say *whom* we feel to be our antithesis – the theologians and all that has theologian blood in its veins – our entire philosophy ... So long as the priest, that denier, calumniator and poisoner of life by *profession*, still counts as a *higher* kind of human being, there can be no answer to the question: what *is* truth?".[86]

Friedrich Nietzsche's revolt against the system of values established by men of resentment is actually a struggle for the recognition of the value of his own personality. "What a theologian feels to be true *must* be false: this provides almost a criterion of truth".[87] The success of Immanuel Kant, Leibniz, Descartes or any other "great man" in European culture is a "theologian's success".[88] Friedrich Nietzsche often argued, in various forms, that metaphysicians are disguised theologians. What are the German philosopher's reproaches against these metaphysicians, of whom he made the terrible declaration that their essence is "*Umwertung aller Werte*"? The answer to this question is essential for the thesis I support in this essay. Friedrich Nietzsche's axioclastic anger against all values has only one motivation:

---

86 Friedrich Nietzsche, *The Antichrist*, pp. 131–132.
87 Ibidem, p. 132.
88 Ibidem, p. 133.

the fact that a man of such high value as he is ignored. As a philosopher, he was completely unknown; the "masters" of this field overlooked him until the last decade of the nineteenth century, when his ascension occurred suddenly, as a revelation, and had the features of a quasi-religious cult.[89] The philosophical destiny of Friedrich Nietzsche, the anti-Christian, is an illustration of the Christian thesis according to which the last shall be first.

During the period when Nietzsche was an exalted apostle of the philosophy of Arthur Schopenhauer, he characterized the German culture as *philistine* because, in Germany, when his master was not completely ignored as a philosopher, he was considered to be simply a dilettante. This degenerate *deutsche Kultur* would recover, Nietzsche thought, when it recognized Arthur Schopenhauer as its own authentic philosopher; his viewpoint on this can be seen in his short paper called *The Relation of Schopenhauer's Philosophy to a German Culture*. After his separation from Arthur Schopenhauer, Nietzsche thought as follows: not only German culture, but the whole of European culture is *philistine*, meaning that it is not being produced by the sons of Muses, but by *philistines* who only pretend to possess inspiration, passion and genius. Philistine culture was decadent, degenerate, sick. We could speak of its recovery only when we began to speak of Friedrich Nietzsche as its greatest and maybe its only philosopher.

"The lowest orders, the *underworld* of the ancient world",[90] secured the victory for the man of resentment. He won not only because of his strength, but also because of his weakness. This immense power of losers over and above men who are really physically and morally powerful was Friedrich Nietzsche's great discovery in terms of the will to power. But because no one recognized his merits, he felt resentment towards these *loser* founders of the Christian European civilization, which had defeated such a giant as the Roman Empire.

Friedrich Nietzsche's hatred of Paul, as seen in *The Antichrist*, is not different from the resentment he attributed to the man of resentment. It must,

---

89 Peter Köster, *Der verbotene Philosoph: Studien zu den Anfängen der katholischen Nietzsche-Rezeption in Deutschland (1890–1918)*, Walter de Gruyter, Berlin, 1998, p. 7.
90 Friedrich Nietzsche, *The Antichrist*, p. 143.

however, be noted that his feeling of hatred for "this *frightful impostor*",[91] as he characterized the Apostle, was repeated and became resentment. Friedrich Nietzsche relives his hatred of Paul at the mere sight of a Christian, as he said himself in *The Antichrist*: "There are days when I am haunted by a feeling blacker than the blackest melancholy – *contempt of man*. And so as to leave no doubt as to *what* I despise, *whom* I despise: it is the man of today, the man with whom I am fatefully contemporary. The man of today – I suffocate of his impure breath".[92]

Friedrich Nietzsche attributes his own failure on all levels to the fact that the Christian world, founded by men of resentment, is unable to recognize true values. "In this world even the finest things amount to nothing without someone to make a show of them: great men the people call these showmen. Little do the people comprehend what is great, which is: the creative. But they do have a sense for all showmen and play-actors of great matters".[93] It goes without saying that in such passages Friedrich Nietzsche was speaking about himself. His work was not taken into account because he refused to be an *arranger* or to turn to the services of a *chief of statute labour*. He was also the creator of authentic values that a society shaped by counterfeit values refused to recognize. Any sentiment, and especially *le ressentiment*, cannot be described properly if you do not experience it yourself. How could anyone describe the sentiment of sacral as Rudolf Otto, for instance, did, if he himself did not have religious sentiments? The same goes for resentment. Friedrich Nietzsche was himself deeply marked by resentment so that the *knowledge* that he offered about this very complex experience is, rather, *self-knowledge*.

3. The Germans are hell

As is well known, some authors consider that, when preparing his last writings, *Ecce Homo* and *The Antichrist*, Friedrich Nietzsche was still in full possession of his senses; others, on the contrary, believe that, despite the coherence of the ideas they contain and their charming style, these two

---

91 Ibidem, p. 172.
92 Ibidem, p. 161.
93 Friedrich Nietzsche, *Thus Spoke Zarathustra*, p. 45.

works were developed after he had already become gone mad. An extreme position in this respect is represented, among others, by Max Nordau, who believed that not only *Ecce Homo* and *The Antichrist* but all of Nietzsche's work is proof of his inherent insanity.

For the thesis we support in this essay it is important to note that these last works of Nietzsche's are typical of what he himself called creation from resentment. In *Antichrist*, he expressed unequivocally his deep resentment of Christianity, while *Ecce Homo* is about his deep resentment of Germans. These are, for Friedrich Nietzsche, hell itself. In no other of his works are his criticisms of his compatriots as resentful as in *Ecce Homo*.

In early December 1888, Friedrich Nietzsche composed a letter to Otto von Bismarck in which he announced to him that he would send the first copy of *Ecce Homo*, as a sign of his hatred, signing it *"Der Antichrist Friedrich Nietzsche"*.[94] He had nourished immeasurable ambitions since childhood, so it is no wonder that they took a downright pathological shape towards the end of life. Using a beautiful expression of Giovanni Papini's, I would say that he wanted to be everything and ended up being nothing, if we refer only to the period before his final mental collapse. After this period, the "myth of Nietzsche" arose suddenly, but this myth has little to do with what is human, all too human, in the philosopher's being. *Ecce Homo*, written in 1888 but published only in 1908, aroused keen interest from various categories of researchers, who were trying to decipher Friedrich Nietzsche's mental illnesses in his writing. He "always felt in the role of a Messiah and believed that the balance of the world rested on his shoulders. He spoke as an Atlas of the pen".[95] In a letter to Brandes, dated 20 November 1888, the German philosopher announced the completion of his book *Ecce Homo*, which would be, he said, like a piece of heavy artillery targeting Christianity. As an old gunner, Nietzsche said in that letter that he would use the idea of *Umwertung aller Werte* to produce convulsions across the entire world.[96] What this "old gunner" forgot to say is that his

---

94 Anacleto Verrecchia, *Zarathustras Ende. Die Katastrophe Nietzsches in Turin*, Böhlaus Verlag, Wien, 1986, p. 9.
95 Anacleto Verrecchia, *Zarathustras Ende. Die Katastrophe Nietzsches in Turin*, p. 165.
96 Ibidem, pp. 169–170.

military career had come to a lamentable end when he simply fell off a horse. He had never forgotten this humiliation and now, in the twilight, took revenge by using his books as if they were guns directed particularly against Christianity and against his homeland, Germany.

In a letter to Strindberg, of 8 December 1888, Friedrich Nietzsche stated that *Ecce Homo* was a deeply anti-German book. The first copies would be sent to the Chancellor Otto von Bismarck and the Kaiser, accompanied by a declaration of war.[97] "I am strong enough to divide the world into two pieces. There remains the problem of translation into English. Do you have a proposal in this regard? An anti-German book in England!".[98] Such texts are the clearest expression of the fact that *Ecce Homo* is the furious reaction of its author's resentment towards the German culture. Using military language, the philosopher expressed his conviction that this book is the dynamite that would blow up all the values of German culture. *Umwertung aller Werte* means now, above all, the reversal of all German values. If Germany did not recognize Friedrich Nietzsche as one of its highest values, it meant that this *Kultur* was *entartet* and must disappear. *Ecce Homo* was, in the exalted imagination of its author, the bomb that would form the death blow and would really divide the history of Germany, of Europe and even the whole world into two distinct eras: before and after Friedrich Nietzsche. He would be the new saviour after whom a new count of the years would start and thus he would finally be recognized by Germany as a leading value of its culture.

The new hierarchy of values would have Friedrich Nietzsche at the top. These are not all simply metaphors, but elements of the scenario imagined by the philosopher who, at least semi-consciously, always harboured the hope that the last would be first. He is the man of resentment, such as may rarely be seen throughout history. "Freedom from ressentiment, enlightenment over ressentiment – who knows the extent to which I ultimately owe thanks to my protracted sickness for this too! Ressentiment is... his most natural inclination. – This was grasped by that profound physiologist Buddha. His "religion", which one would do better to call a system of hygiene so as not to mix it up with such pitiable things as Christianity, makes its

---

97 Ibidem, p. 175.
98 Ibidem, p. 175.

effect dependent on victory over ressentiment: to free the soul of that – first step to recovery. "Not by enmity is enmity ended, by friendship is enmity ended": this stands at the beginning of Buddha's teaching".[99] However, Nietzsche himself died as a staunch opponent of Christianity, as a mortal enemy of the German culture, as a misanthrope full of contempt for mankind, as he said himself in the short *Preface* to *The Antichrist*.

Many times, Friedrich Nietzsche wished to assure his readers that he kept aloof from any desire for revenge when a reckless act was directed towards him. But this is only a mask to hide the sentiment of hatred against someone who humiliates you by overshadowing you in terms of value: a typical reaction of the man of resentment. In fact, Friedrich Nietzsche sought to take revenge through his book on all those who did not recognize his own value – that is, as he said himself in *Ecce Homo*, most of his contemporaries: "But the disparity between the greatness of my task and the smallness of my contemporaries has found expression in the fact that I have been neither heard nor even so much as seen".[100] Beyond the mania of grandiosity, from which Friedrich Nietzsche undoubtedly suffered, he recognized that no one paid him attention as a philosopher, as a philologist, as a writer, as a moralist or in any of the many roles he assigned himself. His *shadow* was always the failure. It accompanied him everywhere and amplified ever more as the night of the mind drew closer. It is no coincidence that *Ecce Homo* started with the evocation of his work *The Wanderer and His Shadow* and also with a reference to the year 1879 when, he said, he gave up his chair at the University of Basel. In reality, he was forced to give up the position of university professor. A number of factors led to this result, but it was certainly not simply the philosopher's *choice*, as he insinuated whenever he referred to the end of his university career. His departure from Basel represented his failure as a teacher, a failure that would exacerbate his resentment for everything connected with German academia. His claims in *Ecce Homo* about the success he had enjoyed when he taught Greek at the University of Basel were not founded in reality. But they prove that Basel obsessed him

---

99   Friedrich Nietzsche, *Ecce Homo*, available at https://archive.org/details/The CompleteWorksOfFriedrichNietzschevol.17-EcceHomo. Accessed February 28, 2016.
100 Ibidem.

as the place where his own decadence started. When he said that he never tried for honours, Friedrich Nietzsche brought again into question the fact that, at 24 years of age, he had been appointed professor at Basel, even if he never wanted it. "I cannot remember ever having taken any trouble – no trace of struggle can be discovered in my life, I am the opposite of an heroic nature. To "want" something, to "strive" after something, to have a "goal", a "wish" in view – I know none of this from experience".[101] In this regard, his entire body of work contradicts him. Like any resentful man, Friedrich Nietzsche did not recognize his failure or his wish for revenge against those who he belived had caused this failure.

The Germans, who should have been the first to recognize a genius like Friedrich Nietzsche, were for him the most unlikeable of all earthlings. There were, however, even among Germans, a few exceptions, such as Professor Friedrich Ritschl, who venerated him, considering him "the only scholar gifted with genius whom I have encountered up to the present day. He was characterized by that pleasant depravity which distinguishes us Thuringians and which can render even a German sympathetic".[102] There are other examples of likeable Germans to whom Nietzsche referred, the feature common to all of them being the fact that they appreciated Friedrich Nietzsche.

Nietzsche's vehement rejection of idealism is also a resentful reaction against Germans. In the chapter *The Case of Wagner. A Musician's Problem* in *Ecce Homo* he repeated, like a litany, "Without any doubt the Germans are idealists".[103] The idea that the philosopher's resentment of Germans came from his failure in the German culture is not a simplistic interpretation or pure speculation, but a truth supported by all Friedrich Nietzsche's work and his conduct in life. For him, all famous Germans are idealists, which meant those suspected of intellectual and moral dishonesty. "Every great cultural crime of four centuries is what they have on their conscience! ... And always from the same cause, from their most inherent cowardice in the face of reality, which is also cowardice in the face of truth, from the falseness which has become instinct with them, from "idealism"".[104] If Germans have

---

101 Ibidem.
102 Ibidem.
103 Ibidem.
104 Ibidem.

committed so many cultural crimes, such as the restoration of Christianity by Martin Luther when he was almost defeated, they will not back away from the highest possible crime: ignoring an overwhelming destiny like that of Friedrich Nietzsche. "The readers and auditors most natural to me are still Russians, Scandinavians and French – will they always be so? – In the history of knowledge the Germans are represented by nothing but ambiguous names, they have ever produced only "unconscious" false-coiners (– Fichte, Schelling, Schopenhauer, Hegel, Schleiermacher deserve this description as well as Kant and Leibniz; they are all mere Schleiermacher, mere veilmakers –): they ought never to have the honour of harbouring the first honest spirit in the history of the spirit, the spirit in whom truth comes to judgement on the false-coinage of four millennia".[105] Friedrich Nietzsche's xenophilia was determined by the fact that foreigners appreciated him more than the Germans. "I cannot endure this race, with which one is always in bad company, which has no finger for *nuances* – woe is me! I am a *nuance*".[106] As one can easily notice from such passages, it is not Germans who were Nietzsche's fundamental problem, but himself. This resentment he typically felt for his compatriots emanated from the fact that he, the philologist, the psychologist, the moralist, the composer, in short, the creator of values, meant nothing in German culture. An "absurd silence", he said, circles the name of Friedrich Nietzsche. This conspiracy of silence of the German cultural space was interpreted by him as a sure sign of the value of his own work and of the authentic nobility of his character. "The Germans ... They feel free to discuss everything, they even consider themselves decisive, I fear they have even decided about me ... My whole life is the proof de rigueur of these propositions. I seek in it in vain for a single sign of tact, of délicatesse towards me. From Jews yes, never yet from Germans".[107]

If it happened that a few of his German friends expressed appreciation for his books, Nietzsche immediately suspected them of falseness and reproached them for not having had the curiosity to read even one page of his work. The process of *Umwertung aller Werte* was primarily aimed at the Germans because only they were able to venerate "a Cagliostro of the

---

105 Ibidem.
106 Ibidem.
107 Ibidem.

music", as Richard Wagner is called in *Ecce Homo*, and to ignore the only truly honest creator of German culture, as Nietzsche described himself. The superman is an axioclast because he revaluated all values and reclassified them with Friedrich Nietzsche's work as the axiologic standard. Zarathustra, the herald of the superman, "says that it was knowledge of precisely the good, the "best", which made him feel horror at man in general; it was out of this repugnance that the wings grew which "carried him to distant futures" – he does not dissemble that it is precisely in relation to the good that his type of man, a relatively superman type, is superman, that the good and just would call his superman a devil".[108]

How would the perfect world look from the perspective of the superman? The answer to this question is given by Nietzsche himself in *Ecce Homo*: "The essay "Wagner in Bayreuth" is a vision of my future; on the other hand, in "Schopenhauer as Educator" it is my innermost history, my evolution that is inscribed. Above all my solemn vow!".[109] This is yet more proof that Friedrich Nietzsche always wrote about himself. *Schopenhauer as educator* does not mean anything other than *Nietzsche as educator*, as he said himself in *Ecce Homo*. The world would cease to be meaningless only when it accepted Nietzsche as its educator. His entire struggle for *Umwertung aller Werte* was guided by the hidden intention to re-hierarchize values so that he could stand above all others.

---

108 Ibidem.
109 Ibidem.

IV. Nihilism as Axiological Illness[110]

1. The Savior as *idiot*

Nihilism as a cultural phenomenon is associated with a form of madness or with other illnesses of the human spirit, or is considered an illness itself. The nihilist is not in his right mind or suffers from a strange illness that cannot be diagnosed or treated by any physician. These activities are the responsibility of another type of physician, a 'physician of culture' as Friedrich Nietzsche said.

The nihilist, who knows by certitude that there is nothing behind any recognized and traditional values, has been seen in history as a lunatic, barbarian, out of his mind, or idiotic. In the following lines I will refer to this final state, using as a starting point Nietzsche's strange opinion about the psychological type of Jesus. Nietzsche polemized with Renan, who 'has introduced the two most inappropriate concepts possible into his explanation of the Jesus type: the concept of *genius* and the concept of the *hero* (*héros*)'.[111] Nietzsche's criticism has very strong fundaments. Jesus' psychological features are opposed to those of the hero.

"And even more, what a misunderstanding is the word 'genius'! Our whole concept, our cultural concept, of 'spirit' has no meaning whatever in the world in which Jesus lived. Spoken with the precision of a physiologist, even an entirely different word would still be more nearly fitting here than the word *idiot*."[112]

Oly a misunderstanding caused the word 'idiot' to be excluded by some editors and this action was governed by the idea that using this word would commit blasphemy, or that it was just a bad formulation of a poor lunatic as was Nietzsche's case in his last years. Nietzsche referred to Jesus as a psychological type of idiot not only in his *The Anti-Christ*, but also in other writings. When Nietzsche said that Jesus is an idiot he referred to the fact

---

110 This essay was originally published in *Cultura. International Journal of Philosophy of Culture and Axiology*, vol. VI, 2/2009, pp. 85–107.

111 Friedrich Nietzsche, *The Anti-Christ* in Walter Kaufmann (ed.), *The Portable Nietzsche*, Penguin Books, New York, 1988, p. 600.

112 Ibidem, p. 601.

that Jesus is more than hero and genius together. In this context 'idiot' has no pejorative signification. It is obvious that Nietzsche, the philologist, did not use this word randomly to designate the psychological type of Jesus. There are two motivations for this option: first it is well known that even the people close to Jesus, as we can read in *The New Testament*, considered Jesus as a 'mad' man (Mark, 3: 21)[113]; and, second, when Nietzsche named Jesus, as spiritual type, an *idiot*, he was referring, as it is known in scientific literature, to Dostoevsky's novel *The Idiot*. The Prince, Myshkin, childishly believed in the victory of good in the world, in beauty as a force that will change the world, and in what is generally named *value*.

Speaking from an axiological point of view, Jesus, Don Quixote, prince Myshkin or any other authentic idealist is not ill; on the contrary, they symbolize the health of spirit, the normality of axiological consciousness, the capacity to perceive the highest values. Truly ill are those people who laugh at these 'idiots'. Indeed, Nietzsche said that 'there was only one Christian, and he died on the cross'[114]. The world of *The Gospels* is a sick world, 'as in a Russian novel, a world in which the scum of society, nervous disorders, and "childlike" idiocy seem to be having a rendezvous'[115]. Especially preoccupied by the psychological type of Messiah as it really was, not how he was transformed by the human, too human motivations of the first Christians, Nietzsche noted: "It is regrettable that a Dostoevsky did not live near this most interesting of all decadents – I mean someone who would have known how to sense the very stirring charm of such a mixture of the sublime, the sickly and the childlike."[116]

Referring to Jesus as an idiot, Nietzsche had in mind the fascination of the reader for Prince Myshkin, *the idiot* created by Dostoevsky, fascination which results from the bizarre mix of sublime, illness and childlike. Even those who read Dostoevsky's writings for the first time can easily see that Prince Myshkin is always considered as behaving like a child and that is the main reproach addressed to him. As an example: "There was a special

---

113   Holy Bible - Douay-Rheims, Translated by Richard Challoner, Baronius Press. 2005.
114   Nietzsche, *The Anti-Christ*, p. 612.
115   Ibidem, p. 603.
116   Ibidem.

feature in the prince, consisting of the extraordinary naivety of the attention with which he always listened to something that interested him, and of the replies he gave when he was addressed with questions about it. His face and even the attitude of his body somehow reflected this naivety, this faith, suspecting neither mockery nor humor."[117]

This paper centers on these types of men who in their innocent belief in values behave like children. Dostoevsky's idiot, like Jesus, understood very well what happened when laughter arose wherever he went. 'There are certain ideas, there are lofty ideas, which I ought not to start talking about, because I'll certainly make everyone laugh'.[118] It is obvious that Nietzsche was thinking of Dostoevsky's character when he said that Jesus was neither hero nor genius, but an idiot.

All of this discussion about the bizarre mix of sublimity, illness and childishness, which transform *the idiot* into *the savior* of humanity, is haunted by another extraordinary character of European culture: Don Quixote de La Mancha. The influence of Cervantes' novel on German literature and philosophy is well known. The Romantics were seduced by the character of Don Quixote. "Friedrich and August Schlegel, L. Tieck, Schelling and Jean Paul have named Cervantes a precursor (Vorreiter) of The Romantic movement. Cervantes was celebrated as prototype of the Romantic author... All Romantics, from Brentano, Armin, Novalis, Eichendorff, Kleist, Chamisso, Hofmann to Heine wrote having in mind this source."[119] Even philosophers such as Kant, Fichte, Schleiermacher, Hegel and Schopenhauer were preoccupied by the fantastic world of Don Quixote[120], and the Romantics considered Cervantes' novel a philosophical text.[121]

---

117 Fiodor M. Dostoievski, 2009. *Idiotul* (Bucureşti: Editura Adevărul Holding), vol. II, p. 21. For the english translation of the text it was used Fyodor M. Dostoevsky, 2003. *The idiot* (Vintage), translated by Richard Pevear and Larissa Volokhonsky.

118 Ibidem, p. 28.

119 Anton Dieterich, *Miguel de Cervantes. Mit Selbstzeugnissen und Bilddokumenten*, Rowohlt Verlag, Hamburg, 1984, p. 126.

120 Ibidem.

121 Sebastien Neumeister, *Der romantische Don Quijote*, in vol.: *Miguel de Cervantes' Don Quijote. Explizite und implizite Diskurse im "Don Quijote"*, hrsg. von Christoph Strosetzki, Schmidt Verlag, Berlin: 2005, p. 310.

The philosophical content, more exactly the axiological one, of the novel *Don Quixote*[122], was underlined by Turghenev in a lecture called *Hamlet and Don Quixote*, in January 10, 1860. As a result of the publication of his novel *Fathers and Sons*, Turghenev was considered for a long time the man who brought the concept of *nihilism* into the minds of his contemporaries. For him Don Quixote was 'before everything else the belief, the belief in something eternal... in truth, which is situated out of man'.[123] When he worked at his well known novel *The Idiot*, Dostoevsky also said that 'there is no book deeper ... then *Don Quixote*. This book is till this day the last and the greatest word of the human spirit'.[124] So, the idea that when Nietzsche said Jesus is an idiot he did not refer just to Dostoevsky's *idiot* but also to Cervantes' character is no speculation. In the imagination of the Russian author, Prince Myshkin is a mix between Jesus and Don Quixote, and this aspect is amplified in the manner in which Nietzsche understands *The Idiot*. More than anyone else, Nietzsche had the power and the art to read this novel and not by chance he said that Dostoevsky is 'the only psychologist, incidentally, from whom I had something to learn; he ranks among the most beautiful strokes of fortune in my life, even more than my discovery of Stendhal'.[125]

Let us return to the *idiot*'s naivety, to which Nietzsche refers in his speech about the psychological type of Jesus and let us think just for a few seconds with *Redlichkeit*, as Nietzsche said, with honesty. Imagine that in our world comes a Christian, a man animated by Jesus' values. We must confess that this will be a bizarre appearance, which, if he could survive enough time, would bring laughter wherever he may go. On the world scene this character would not be more different than Don Quixote or Prince Myshkin. So, let us imagine that this man would not just say, but he would truly believe and live according to the following expressions: 'Love your enemies: do good to them that hate you: and pray for them that persecute

122   Nicolae Râmbu, 2008. 'Axiological Reflections about Don Quijote' in *Cultura. International Journal of Philosophy of Culture and Axiology*, no. 10, pp. 65–79.
123   Turgheniev, *Hamlet und Don Quijote*, apud Anton Dietrich, *op. cit.*, p. 127.
124   Anton Dieterich, *Miguel de Cervantes*, p. 127.
125   Friedriech Nietzsche, *Twilght of the Idols* in Walter Kaufmann (ed.), *The Portable Nietzsche*, Penguin Books, New York, 1988, p. 549.

and calumniate you' (Matthew, 5:44) or 'But I say to you not to resist evil: but if one strike thee on thy right cheek, turn to him also the other' (Matthew, 5:39). Leaving beside the fact that this man would not survive a single day, he will be immediately pointed out and considered an idiot, or 'poor in spirit'. When he traced the lines of Jesus' character, Nietzsche thought about this type of man.

'Where my honesty (*meine Redlichkeit*) ceases, I am blind and I also want to be blind.'[126] To translate what Nietzsche named *Redlichkeit* as honesty or sincerity is too little. Dostoevsky's hero, Prince Myshkin, is profoundly *redlich*: "I decided to do my duty honestly and firmly. Maybe it will be boring and painful for me to be with people. In the first place I decided to be polite and candid with everybody; no one can ask more of me. Maybe I'll be considered a child here, too—so be it! Everybody also considers me an idiot for some reason, and in fact I was once so ill that I was like an idiot; but what sort of idiot am I now, when I myself understand that I'm considered an idiot?"[127]

From an axiological perspective he is not an idiot, but the only lucid man, the last human being in a world of non-humans. All the others are possessed by duplicity-hypocrites, mean, insincere, plotters, profiteers without scruples, especially after they heard he was the heir of an important wealth. Myshkin, as any idealist, was a child that believed in stories that always end with the victory of good. All those who stopped laughing and tried to understand the poor 'idiot' remarked his *naivety* and his *sincerity*.[128] He is such an 'idiot', so 'poor in spirit' that he believes that people will appreciate him for his beliefs in values, but, as in the case of Don Quixote, only because he was doing good from the goodness of his heart, everybody thought that he was insane. Instead of being illuminated by the values that he brought, Nastásya Filippovna said to him: 'Well, that's...out of some novel! That, my darling prince, is old gibberish, the world's grown smarter now, and that's all nonsense!'[129] She accepted this sort of 'gibberish' when she found

---

126 Friedrich Nietzsche, *Thus spoke Zarathustra* in Walter Kaufmann (ed.), *The Portable Nietzsche*, Penguin Books, New York, 1988, p. 363.
127 Fiodor M. Dostoievski, *Idiotul*, p. 137.
128 Ibidem.
129 Ibidem, vol. I., p. 212.

out that the Prince had become the heir of a fabulous inheritance: "I'm a princess myself now, you heard it – the prince won't let anyone offend me! Afanasy Ivanovich, congratulate me; now I'll be able to sit next to your wife anywhere; it's useful to have such a husband, don't you think? A million and a half, and a prince, and, they say, an idiot to boot, what could be better? Only now does real life begin!"[130]

To sincerely wish with *Redlichkeit* the happiness of a person, without any interest, without wanting anything from this world and from the next life is a desire of an 'idiot' man. When Nietzsche named Jesus an 'idiot' he surely had in mind the character created by Dostoevsky and the latter was haunted by Don Quixote when wrote his book. Myshkin sent a note to Agláya Ivánovna. She was "dropping the letter into her desk drawer. The next day she took it out again and put it into a thick, sturdily bound book (as she always did with her papers, so as to find them quickly when she needed them). And only a week later did she happen to notice what book it was. It was *Don Quixote de La Mancha*. Agláya laughed terribly—no one knew why."[131]

Like Don Quixote, Myshkin is a man full of virtues who sees the world through his naivety and his generosity and this is why Elizavéta (Lizavéta) Prokófyevna said to him: 'Everyone considers you a fool and deceives you!'.

Some academic papers take up the relation between Nietzsche and Dostoevsky for those who want to find more about it. I want to emphasize the idea that from an axiological point of view health and illness have different significations from those traditionally associated with them, and the idiot, as a psychological type of Jesus, is a significant example.

2. Blessed are those who are poor in spirit? An axiological interpretation of a mysterious expresion

Using as an assumption Nietzsche's idea of idiot, the psychological type of Jesus and Don Quixote, I present a new interpretation of the following expression as it appears in *The Bible*: 'Blessed are the poor in spirit: for theirs is the kingdom of heaven'. (Matthew, 5:3). Every one of us has difficulties

---

130 Ibidem, p. 218.
131 Ibidem, p. 243.

understanding the meaning of this enunciation. In fact, to be *redlich*, honest, we must recognize that this enunciation has no meaning, not just from the side of the Christian values but also from that of any values. An axiological conscience can not accept 'the poor in spirit' as a positive value.

From a novel axiological point of view, the expression 'the poor in spirit' and the whole enunciation about their happiness, which does not accord with the values imposed by Jesus, receives a new and different meaning. Redemption will be offered only to those 'poor in spirit', to idiots, as Nietzsche defined them. Only those who live according to the values brought by Jesus, those who are considered idiots by the rest of the world, will be redeemed. 'When Nietzsche characterized Jesus as an idiot, he did not do that with an insulting intention. By idiot Nietzsche understood – following the essential signification of the Greek term – an apolitical man who stands far away from public business.'[132] Nietzsche, in the context of considering Jesus an idiot, had in mind more than a person who is not interested in politics matters and who is not involved in the public life. In Nietzsche's view, Jesus symbolizes moral purity, so he cannot represent for others anything other than an idiot. The man who stands opposite to Jesus is Paul, the true founder of Christianity, who was fiercely criticized by Nietzsche. He is absolutely not an idiot, as Nietzsche mentioned in a note from 1888.[133] The whole array of features that characterizes Jesus, his childish and sublime charm, is missing in Saint Paul's personality. "On the heels of the 'glad tidings' came the very worst: those of Paul. In Paul was embodied the opposite type to that of the 'bringer of glad tidings': the genius in hatred, in the vision of hatred, in the inexorable logic of hatred. *How much* this dysangelist sacrificed to hatred!"[134] In Nietzsche's view, Paul is the main person responsible for the corruption of Christianity, for its orientation in an opposite direction to that indicated by Jesus.

As we know from the Gospel of Mark, even Jesus' family and friends considered him mad, 'He is become mad' (Mark, 3:21). We must not look

---

132 Hans-Jürgen Gawoll, *Nihilismus und Metaphysik. Entwicklungsgeschichtliche Untersuchung vom deutschen Idealismus bis zu Heidegger*, Frommann-Holzboog Verlag, Stuttgart, 1989, p. 182.
133 Ibidem.
134 Friedrich Nietzsche, *The Anti-Christ*, p. 617.

for occult significations. Every one who behaves today according to the original Christian values will be considered as 'becoming mad', as 'idiot'. We must differentiate two types of attitudes about Christianity in Nietzsche: a profound admiration for the values brought by Jesus and a tough criticism of perverted Christianity, especially regarding Saint Paul's writings. Modern values, based on corrupted Christianity, and having pity as their center, are *nihilistic* values'.[135] Following Schopenhauer, Nietzsche said that 'pity negates life and renders it more *deserving of negation*. Pity is *the practice* of nihilism'.[136] Through pity evil appears in the world, values lose their power because the law of natural selection is not respected and what must disappear continues to live and what must live disappears.

"In our whole unhealthy modernity there is nothing unhealthier than Christian pity. To be physicians *here*, to be inexorable *here*, to wield the scalpel *here* – that is *our* part, that is *our* love of man, that is how *we* are philosophers, we *Hyperboreans*."[137] A world in which pity stays is, in its axiological center, evolving towards nihilism.

Christianity, in the way it imposed itself in history, brought a sudden overthrow of Jesus' values and this happened through shrewdness[138], through abusive interpretation of Jesus' words. For Nietzsche, the expressions used in the *Gospels* are the symptoms of a very bad corruption that appeared in the first Christian community and than spread to all of Christianity. "One cannot read these Gospels cautiously enough; every word poses difficulties. I confess – one will pardon me – that precisely on this account they are a first-rate delight for a psychologist – as the opposite of all naïve corruption, as subtlety par excellence, as artistry in psychological corruption. The Gospels stand apart."[139]

How must we read the enunciation 'Blessed are the poor in spirit: for theirs is the kingdom of heaven' in order to understand it well? For Nietzsche, the philologist, 'the kingdom of heaven' "is a state of the heart – not something that is to come 'above the earth or 'after death'…The 'kingdom

135 Ibidem, p. 572.
136 Ibidem, p. 573.
137 Ibidem, p. 574.
138 Ibidem, p. 582.
139 Ibidem, p. 620.

of God' is nothing that one expects; it has no yesterday – and no day after tomorrow, it wilt not come in 'a thousand years' – it is an experience of the heart; it is everywhere, it is nowhere."[140]

The corruption of Christianity is translated also into the interpretation of the concept of life after death as we can see in all interpreters and commentators from all kinds of Christian denominations. Both 'the kingdom of heaven' and 'the happiness' were understood differently from what Jesus wanted to transmit. Nietzsche repeats in his writings the idea that what Jesus had affirmed, his Christian successors had negated and what he had negated these had affirmed.[141] The values he had negated are very well known: those of war, including self-defense, judging others, differences between nations and social classes, the anger, hatred, and disdain; but the Christians became themselves soldiers, judges, merchants, theologians, priests, philosophers, kings or emperors.[142] The church became the opposite of what Jesus preached. The Christians, as Nietzsche said, repeated Jesus' words 'Judge not, that you may not be judged' (Matthew, 7:1) but they still 'consign to hell everything that stands in their way'.[143] Such overthrow of values through an abusive interpretation is a premise of nihilism, of the belief that behind each value stands nothing.

Saint Paul, as Nietzsche believed, instead of being an apostle of love, was one of hatred and revenge. "Indeed, one cannot be a philologist or physician without at the same time being an *anti-Christian*. For as a philologist one sees behind the 'holy books', as a physician, behind the physiological depravity of the typical Christian. The physician says 'incurable'; the philologist 'swindle'."[144]

Let us return now to the puzzling enunciation 'Blessed are the poor in spirit: for theirs is the kingdom of heaven', puzzling because the values that it affirms are not those preached by Jesus. Nietzsche mentioned that happiness is not related to some conditions, less to the condition of being 'poor in

---

140 Ibidem, p. 608.
141 Hermann L. Goldschmidt, *Der Nihilismus im Licht einer kritischen Philosophie*, Europäische Verlagsanstalt, Frankfurt am Main, 1941, p. 25.
142 Ibidem, p. 26.
143 Nietzsche, *The Anti-Christ*, p. 621.
144 Ibidem, p. 628.

spirit'; on the contrary, happiness is the only reality, in other words a state, a *practice*. Happy is that one who "is distinguished by acting differently: by not resisting, either in words or in his heart, those who treat him ill; by making no distinction between foreigner and native, between Jew and not-Jew ('the neighbor' – really the coreligionist, the Jew); by not growing angry with anybody, by not despising anybody; by not permitting himself to be seen or involved at courts of law ('hot swearing'); by not divorcing his wife under any circumstances, not even if his wife has been proved unfaithful. All of this, at bottom one principle; all of this, consequences of one instinct. The life of the Redeemer was nothing other than *this* practice – nor was his death anything else."[145]

Having in mind the signification of this *practice*, the meaning of the puzzling enunciation could be 'Blessed are the idiots', following Nietzsche's interpretation, 'for theirs is the kingdom of heaven'. There are many passages in *The Bible* where 'the authentic Christian practice' is considered to be something only an idiot could do. I offer here just one example: 'But the sensual man perceived not these things that are of the Spirit of God; for it is foolishness to him' (1st. Corinthians, 2:14). In *The Anti-Christ*, Nietzsche made the idiot's portrait and this portrait suits Jesus, Prince Myshkin and all idealists whenever they lived and who, as Plato said, are 'going to act prudently in private or in public'[146], being more attracted by the noumena, their souls looking at those things above.

3. Philosophy as convalescence treatise

If Nietzsche saw everywhere '*sick* spirits', 'epileptics of the concept', 'sick reason' and saw the Church as 'the catholic madhouse', could not we assume that he was mad not only when he was hospitalized in Jena but even in his entire life? Could not the fact that he easily considered Saint Paul's words as 'the talk of a lunatic' be a sign of his own madness? Are not 'The mental illnesses' of the Christian church and 'the madhouse world of the whole millennia' of Christianity, mentioned in *The Anti-Christ*, signs of the place where Nietzsche himself finally arrived?

---

145 Ibidem, pp. 606–7.
146 Plato, *The Republic* (Basic Books), translated by Allan Bloom, 1991, 517 c.

In the following lines I elucidate the problem of Nietzsche's illnesses. On one side there are authors like Gottfried Benn, saying that the subject of 'Nietzsche and his illness' has no signification for Nietzsche's philosophical work and if would have died in 1980, his work would remain the same today.[147] On the other side some authors mention the fact that Nietzsche's madness is not a late appearance in his life and the reality is that he was never mentally healthy. In his *Entartung*, Max Nordau has a whole chapter about Nietzsche, considering that Nietzsche's philosophy is a degenerate one, an expression of a mentally sick man. When you read Nietzsche's writings, said Nordau, you have the impression that those pages were written by an angry madman. His whole work is the expression of a delirium. He wanted at any price to impose his fixations; that is why he proclaimed, like a tyrant, instead of demonstrating or arguing an idea. It is not a surprise that he constantly contradicts himself on the same page. When he realized this, as Nordau observed, Nietzsche said that he wanted to amuse himself, deceiving the readers: "It is hard to be understood … and you should give heartfelt thanks for the goodwill apparent in any subtlety of interpretation. But as far as 'good friends' are concerned, they are always too easy-going and think that they have a right to be easy-going, just because they are friends. So it is best to grant them some leeway from the very start, and leave some latitude for misunderstandings: – and then you can even laugh. Or, alternatively, get rid of them altogether, these good friends, – and then laugh some more!"[148]

On the other hand, as Nordau noted, in Nietzsche's writings there are whole pages which say nothing, being simple affirmations of a madman. *Thus Spoke Zarathustra* is the main paper used by Nordau in order to demonstrate the fact that Friedrich Nietzsche was mentally ill his entire life.

When an idea is clearly presented it is just a platitude formulated in such a manner as to amaze. Nordau offers as example the *Umwertung aller Werte* that was already a commonplace in the history of culture when Nietzsche presented it as a great discovery. Everybody knew that values are periodically reevaluated in history. Nietzsche was original just when he

147 Gottfried Benn, *Nietzsche – Nach fünfzig Jahren* in *Essays, Reden, Vorträge*, Limes Verlag, Wiesbaden, 1962, p. 487.
148 Friedrich Nietzsche, *Beyound Good and Evil*, Cambridge University Press, New York, 2002, pp. 28–9.

was in trance, when his speech, very good from the stylistic point of view, did not say anything. All the rest, says Nordau, is obvious triviality. The philosophy of will is too much inspired by Schopenhauer, 'my great master', as Nietzsche named him, 'to whom that book of mine spoke as though he were still present'.[149] Nietzsche's originality, in Nordau's view, consists in the childish reversal of a rational discourse and his philosophy was born from the obsession to contradict, deny and polemicize against everybody and on every subject. All these are symptoms of Nietzsche's mental illness. In the preface of *The Genealogy of Morality* Nietzsche said that he was inspired by Paul Rée's *The Origin of Moral Sensations*. Even Paul Rée's ideas seemed to be strange; Nietzsche wrote: "I was given the initial stimulation to publish something about my hypotheses on the origin of morality by a clear, honest and clever, even too-clever little book, in which I first directly encountered the back-to front and perverse kind of genealogical hypotheses, actually the *English* kind, which drew me to it – with that power of attraction which everything contradictory and antithetical has … I have, perhaps, never read anything to which I said 'no', sentence by sentence and deduction by deduction, as I did to this book: but completely without annoyance and impatience."[150]

Max Nordau mentions that we must not doubt this affirmation because it is according to his philosophical style. It is a typical reaction of a sick mind, affected by the obsession to contradict and negate. In *Gay Science*, where we find the most elaborated presentation of the relation between illness and philosophy, Nietzsche recognizes his own desire to deny: 'my way of thinking requires a warlike soul, a desire to hurt, a delight in saying no'.[151] His obsession to deny is also clearly expressed in *Twilight of the Idols*: 'My taste, which may be the opposite of a tolerant taste, is in this case too far from saying Yes indiscriminately: it does not like to say Yes; rather even No; but best of all, nothing'.[152]

---

149 Friedrich Nietzsche,. *On the Genealogy of Morality*, Cambridge University Press, New York, 2007 , pp. 6–7.

150 Ibidem, pp. 5–6.

151 Friedrich Nietzsche, *The Gay Science*, Cambridge University Press, New York, 2008 , p. 53.

152 Friedrich Nietzsche, *Twilight of the Idols* in Walter Kaufmann (ed.), *The Portable Nietzsche*, Penguin Books, New York, p. 556.

Having as starting point these types of citations, Nordau concludes that Nietzsche had a born perverse predisposition to transform healthy moral inclination into its contrary. He was a madman, but a peaceful one, who never turned to action. His destructive actions were shown only in writing. But in Nietzsche's speech there is something that gives shivers: his cruel philosophical representations are always accompanied by a feeling of pleasure. The specialists, as Nordau reminds us, have a precise word for this type of illness: sadism.[153] In Nietzsche's case the sadism is limited only to the spiritual sphere and its perverse satisfaction is manifested in the ideal field.[154] To sustain this type of hypothesis, Nordau offers in his *Entartung* many excerpts from which cruel images are accompanied by representations of voluptuousness. To exemplify: 'At the centre of all these noble races we cannot fail to see the beast of prey, the magnificent *blond beast* avidly prowling round for spoil and victory'[155] The noble races were also beasts of prey, characterized by 'their unconcern and scorn for safety, body, life, comfort, their shocking cheerfulness and depth of delight in all destruction'.[156] The aversion against man, mentioned repeatedly by Nietzsche, is based on the fact that man is 'out of the beast of prey'.[157] In *The Gay Science* there are some references to 'the voluptuousness of his own hell', the voluptuousness of pain, 'Who will attain something great if he does not feel in himself the power *to inflict* great pain?'[158], about the joy of the dangerous life and the saintly cruelty.

Between 1892 and 1893, when the two volumes of Nordau's *Entartung*, appeared, Friedrich Nietzsche was hospitalized as incurably mad in the hospital headed by Professor Binswagner in Jena.

Why does Max Nordau insist so much on Nietzsche's madness, especially on the fact that he had been born with this illness? The reason is that 'Nietzsche had become the author of a spiritual contamination and to stop this means to reveal his madness'.[159] As an epidemic disease, Nietzsche's

---

153 Max Nordau, 1984. *Dégénérescence*, vol. II, Alcan, Paris, p. 366.
154 Ibidem, p. 367.
155 Friedrich Nietzsche, *On the Genealogy*, p. 23.
156 Ibidem.
157 Ibidem, p. 24.
158 Friedrich Nietzsche, *The Gay Science*, p. 181.
159 Max Nordau, *Dégénérescence*, p. 372.

philosophy had spread very rapidly. The success of his books was seen as a sign of a degenerated world, an ill one. His readers were considered like their preferred author, degenerates and sadists, even if this type of sadism does not surpass the ideal level. From Nordau's point of view, Nietzsche's disciples were alienated.

Madness and *alienation* are too general to define precisely as mental illness. Nietzsche was affected especially by 'maniac exaltation'[160], which was one way he often lost the logical weir of his ideas, not knowing what his starting point was anymore, and finishing the phrase with a false conclusion, which had no connection with the hypothesis he used. Among the examples used by Nordau in the medical interpretation of the philosopher's illness symptoms is the following one: "Hah! Come up, dignity! / Virtuous dignity! European dignity! / Blow, blow again, / Bellows of virtue! / Hah! / Once more roar, / Roar morally! / As a moral lion / Roar before the daughters of the wilderness! / For virtuous howling, / My most charming girls, / Is more than anything else / European fervor, European ravenous hunger. / And there I stand even now / As a European; / I cannot do else; / God help me! / Amen. / *Wilderness grows: woe unto him that harbors wildernesses!*"[161]

Nietzsche's psychic diseases were analyzed in great detail. Here I am interested only in two aspects: first is the quick and alarming propagation of Nietzsche's work through a sort of contamination and second the value of the disease, the extraordinary importance that Nietzsche offered to the disease in the process of creation. It is very true that Nietzsche suffered from many somatic and psychic diseases but the voluptuousness of sufferance, underlined by Max Nordau, was wrongly interpreted. What was left out is the research on Nietzsche's spiritual illnesses. As he recognized himself, it is hard to differentiate between soul (or psyche) and spirit, especially when we talk about illness. "One might guess that I do not want to take my leave ungratefully from that time of severe illness whose profits I have not yet exhausted even today: I am well aware of the advantages that my erratic health gives me over all burly minds. A philosopher who has passed through many kinds of health, and keeps passing through them again and

---

160   Ibidem, p. 378.
161   Nietzsche, *Thus spoke Zarathustra*, p. 421.

again, has passed through an equal number of philosophies; he simply *cannot* but translate his state every time into the most spiritual form and distance – this art of transfiguration just *is* philosophy. We philosophers are not free to separate soul from body as the common people do; we are even less free to separate soul from spirit."[162]

Besides somatic and psychic diseases, Nietzsche suffered together with his epoch from a spiritual illness: nihilism. This is a strange illness and on this particular one I want to keep an eye. Some confusions and false interpretations about the praise of disease and the voluptuousness of torture have been born from the interest given only to the somatic and psychic diseases and from the assumption that nihilism is a philosophical doctrine or a *Weltanschauung*. 'Nihilism is not obtained as it is *Weltanschauung*, but you are contaminated by it like a disease.'[163] This affirmation is correct but I must add: it is not a psychical disease as it was characterized by all those who had interpreted nihilism as a disease phenomenon, but an illness of the soul.

The voluptuousness that Nietzsche feels in the face of the overthrow of all values, his great satisfaction in saying *no*, as he confessed in *The Gay Science*, the praise of pain, his cruelty as the great festive joy etc. are easily remarked by any of his readers. If we have in mind the psychosomatic signification of illness, then Nordau's conclusions are impossible to avoid. But for Nietzsche: "Only great pain, that long, slow pain that takes its time and in which we are burned, as it were, over green wood, forces us philosophers to descend into our ultimate depths and put aside all trust, everything good-natured, veiling, mild, average – things in which formerly we may have found our humanity."[164]

The nihilism, the illness that makes us *deeper*[165], is not a psychical illness but a spiritual one and from this point of view, Nietzsche is not a patient but a physician of culture. He did not only diagnose the main illness of the European spirit but also, as a good European, was preoccupied by the

162 Nietzsche, *The Gay Science*, p. 6.
163 Hans Lilje, *Nihilismus*, Furche-Verlag, Tübingen, 1947, p. 24, apud Gerhard Gloege, 'Nihilismus?' in Dieter Arendt (Hrsg.), *Der Nihilismus als Phänomen der Geistesgeschichte in der wissenschaftlichen Diskussion unseres Jahrhunderts*, Wissenschaftliche Buchgesellschaft, Darmstadt, 1974, p. 53.
164 Friedrich Nietzsche, *The Gay Science*, p. 6.
165 Ibidem, p. 7.

defeat of nihilism, its surpassing, and by the capacity to get to 'the great wealth' passing inevitably through 'the great pain'. He becomes what a true philosopher must be: a physician of culture.

In the world of spirit the illness is not necessarily something bad; on the contrary, we must raise our ideas from our pain.[166] Regarding the main cultural illness of Europe, Nietzsche considered that all its creative impulses are born through his sufferance: "Europe is a patient who owes the utmost gratitude to his incurability and to the perpetual changes in his affliction: these incessantly new conditions, these no less incessantly new dangers, pains, and modes of information have finally generated an intellectual irritability that approximates genius and that is in any case the mother of all genius."[167]

The illness is not in Nietzsche's work only a main philosophical category, but it is also an essential part in the process of the reevaluation of all values. To the question: 'Why I am so wise?', 'Why I am so clever?' and 'Why do I write such good books?', which are the names of the first three chapters of his *Ecce Homo*, the answer is the same: because I was so ill that 'a long, all-too-long succession of years meant recuperation for me'.[168] Not only *The Gay Science* but all Nietzsche's philosophy represents a convalescence treatise. "A psychologist knows few questions as attractive as that concerning the relation between health and philosophy; and should he himself become ill, he will bring all of his scientific curiosity into the illness."[169]

He made the panegyric of the illness without making a rigorous distinction between the somatic, psychic and spiritual illnesses. In the same paragraph he referred to the intellectual illnesses but also to the eye, nerve, stomach illnesses and also to decadence, a cultural illness. In fact he suffered only from nihilism, together with his entire epoch, to which he consecrated his scientific curiosity. Only from this point of view we can really understand the following excerpt from *Ecce Homo*: "To be able to look out from the optic of sickness towards *healthier* concepts and values, and again the

---

166 Ibidem.

167 Ibidem, pp. 49–50.

168 Friedrich Nietzsche, *Ecce Homo* in Friedrich Nietzsche, *The Anti-Christ, Ecce Homo, Twilight of the Idols and other writings*, Cambridge University Press, New York, 2006, p. 76.

169 Nietzsche, *The Gay Science*, p. 4.

other way around, to look down from the fullness and self-assurance of the *rich* life into the secret work of the instinct of decadence – that was my longest training, my genuine experience, if I became the master of anything, it was this. I have a hand for switching *perspectives*: the first reason why a 'revaluation of values' is even possible, perhaps for me alone."[170]

Having in mind the fact that Nietzsche further described his own experience as a person suffering from nihilism and elaborated less a theory about nihilism, I consider that it is an error to consider him a philosopher of nihilism. Like Cioran later, named the Balcanic Nietzsche, he is only a nihilist, not a theoretician, a *Wissenschaftler*, of this complex phenomenon. But that is in fact his inconsequentiality as a nihilist.

4. Patients and physicians of culture

Nietzsche's 'sadism', mentioned by Nordau in *Entartung*, is not a very accurate diagnosis. He lived voluptuously the sufferance resulted from nihilism; in everything else, he was a patient like any other.

All Nietzsche's books, especially those referring to nihilism, are written in a medical language: Socrates was fascinating through the fact that he seemed to be a physician, his reason was just a disease, a religious neurosis; the history of the health of European man and the examples can compose a huge list.

The Genealogy of Morality, *The Anti-Christ*, *Nietzsche contra Wagner*, *Ecce homo* and especially the preface of the second edition of *The Gay Science* are sections from a strange 'Convalescence Treatise'.[171] Schopenhauer's morality of compassion was for Nietzsche a symptom of a cultural illness of his time. The philosopher must not 'read' but 'consult', in the same manner as a physician diagnoses and prescribes procedures for recovery. In the value conferred by modern philosophers on compassion, Nietzsche saw "the onset of the final sickness becoming gently, sadly manifest: I understood the morality of compassion, casting around ever wider to catch even philosophers and make them ill, as the most uncanny symptom of our

---

170 Nietzsche, *Ecce Homo*, p. 76.
171 See Ernst Bertram, *Nietzsche. Încercare de mitologie*, Editura Humanitas, Bucureşti, 1998, p. 123.

European culture which has itself become uncanny, as its detour to a new Buddhism? to a new Euro-Buddhism? to – *nihilism*? ..."[172]

When Nietzsche directly referred to nihilism he did not 'write' as a philosopher, but he 'prescribed' procedures as a physician. As we know, the physician makes referrals: to the hospital for illnesses of the body, to the asylum for severe mental illnesses. The philosopher as a physician of culture does the same thing. To eliminate any confusion, I must specify that in this context I am not speaking only about the illnesses of the soul, which were very clearly explained by Kant in his *Anthropology*. If passion, positive or negative, or emotion surpasses some degree, 'the health of the soul' could be reacquired, for example, through Stoic wisdom. Using Kant's expression we may say that the Stoic philosopher could be a good 'physician of the soul'[173]. In *The Gay Science*, Nietzsche was also referring to 'the health of the soul' (*Gesundheit der Seele*), having as starting point Ariston of Chios's idea that 'virtue is the health of the soul'.[174] Nihilism is not an illness of the soul, but of the spirit, or, when we talk about society, an illness of culture. For those who are ill, Nietzsche 'prescribed' procedures in order to reach 'great health'.[175] Especially "anyone whose soul thirsts to experience the whole range of previous values and aspirations, to sail around all the coasts of this 'inland sea' (*Mittelmeer*) of ideals, anyone who wants to know from the adventures of his experience how it feels to be the discoverer or conqueror of an ideal, or to be an artist, a saint, a lawmaker, a sage, a pious man, a soothsayer, an old-style divine loner – any such person needs one thing above all – *great health*."[176]

Those sick with nihilism 'introduce the deadliest poison and skepticism into our trust in life, in man, in ourselves'.[177] What is the physician of culture's prescription for these kinds of patients, through whom nihilism affects

---

172   Friedrich Nietzsche, *On the Genealogy*, p. 7.
173   Immanuel Kant, *Antropologia din perspectivă pragmatică*, Editura Antaios, Bucureşti, 2001, p. 183.
174   Nietzsche, *The Gay Science*, p. 116.
175   Ibidem, p. 246 (& 382), *Thus spoke Zarathustra*, & 2.
176   Friedrich Nietzsche, *The Gay Science*, p. 246.
177   Friedrich Nietzsche, *On the Genealogy*, p. 89.

the entirety of European culture? Their hospitalization in 'madhouses and hospitals of culture' (*Krankenhäuser und Irrenhäuser der Kultur*).[178]

There is an extensive literature regarding the pathological aspect of nihilism. I will offer some examples to underline my idea. In a conference held on January 7, 1946 in Bremen, right after the Second World War, the German philosopher Ludwig Landgrebe spoke about nihilism as a severe illness of the European spirit.

"The illness of which symptoms we must learn to recognize in the present was diagnosed 60 years ago by Friedrich Nietzsche as *European nihilism*. This means that it is not only a German illness. The Occident was and still remains a spiritual unity despite all the differences that appear during the modern period."[179]

It is an illness of European culture but it is also one of the individual person. Nihilism is a major disorder of the axiological conscience, of the way in which we, as human beings, define ourselves referring to values. It is an axiological illness (in the same way as axiological blindness, tyranny of values etc., underlined especially by German authors such as Nicolai Hartmann, Dietrich von Hildebrand, Johannes Hessen) not a psychical one. It is true that this sort of disease can be, at the individual level, accompanied by severe mental diseases: depression, schizophrenia, hysteria etc., but it also can leave unchanged the functions of the human psyche, as Ernst Jünger mentions in his works. A nihilist can be somatically and mentally perfectly healthy. Neurosis, depressions and different kinds of aggression and autoaggression, which could end with suicide, are not caused by nihilism, even though the literature says the contrary.[180]

All those who categorized nihilism in the area of psychical diseases have met insurmountable paradoxes or used ambiguous expressions, like 'psychical-neurotic nihilism' or 'pathological-destructive nihilism'[181],

---

178 Ibidem, p. 92.
179 Ludwig Landsgrebe, "Zur Überwindung des europäischen Nihilismus", in: Dieter Arendt, *Der Nihilismus als Phänomen der Geistesgeschichte in der wissenschaftlichen Diskussion unseres Jahrhunderts*, Wissenschaftliche Buchgesellschaft, Darmstadt, 1974, p. 20.
180 See Wolfgang Kraus, *Nihilismus heute oder die Geduld der Weltgeschichte*, Zsolnay Verlag, Wien & Hamburg, 1983, p. 139.
181 Wolfgang Kraus, op. cit., p. 80.

putting together a psychical and a spiritual illness that do not always occur together.

Including nihilism in the category of axiological illnesses, I hope to offer a way to surpass the dilemmas connected to the interpretation of nihilism as illness. To describe nihilism, to interpret its manifestation, to indicate the ways of surpassing nihilism and to reach 'the great health', all these activities are not for the psychologist or for the psychiatrist, but for the philosopher as physician of culture.

Hermann Rauschning asserts that the first condition to surpass nihilism is the knowledge of its essence. But this is not an easy task. In fact, nihilism 'has no specific form or essence, it could act behind any person or thing. It can be seen only as an effect.'[182] It is always behind a mask, as Rauschning remarks: it can be destructive behind the mask of a creative force, in the way Nietzsche saw it: 'Change of values - that is a change of creators! Who ever must be a creator always annihilates'.[183] Adolf Hitler is a representative example for this 'mask' behind which nihilism appears in history[184], other types of masks being the artist, the reformer etc.

Nihilism, in Rauschning's view, has some elements which can be found in hysteria; this is why the hysterical responses are mixed up in specialized literature with the nihilist ones.[185] Like hysteria, nihilism, as a major disease of the human axiological conscience, is more a way of responding. Both in the case of hysterical and nihilist responses the destructive outbreaks are preceded by a sort of apathy. Even though there are many common points, these two types of responses must not be confounded.[186] It is impossible to establish the type of nihilist[187]; there are different types of hysteria for each type of personality and the same thing is applied to nihilism.

This nihilist's force is the power of the emptiness in a cultural area. As it happens in nature where the vacuum gathers around it great forces, so

---

182 Hermann Rauschning, *Masken und Metamorphosen des Nihilismus. Der Nihilismus des XX. Jahrhunderts*, Humboldt -Verlag, Frankfurt am Main, 1954, p. 7.

183 Friedrich Nietzsche, *Thus spoke Zarathustra*, p. 171.

184 Hermann Rauschning, *Masken und Metamorphosen*, p. 93.

185 Ibidem, pp. 92–3.

186 Ibidem, pp. 91–107.

187 Ibidem, p. 94.

in the world of spirit, taking the place of values, the emptiness also gathers forces, not necessarily destructive ones, but also creative ones, as has been proved by some artistic avant-gardes.

As any other illness, nihilism can be diagnosed, treated, cured. The philosopher as physician of culture is destined to analyze the health of the spirit, to find the patients and to prescribe them prescriptions. Through one of his characters, created for the novel *Crime and Punishment,* Dostoevsky underlined the role of the philosopher in the therapy of the soul: "I'm convinced there are lots of people in Petersburg who talk to themselves as they walk. This is a town of crazy people. If only we have scientific men, doctors, lawyers and philosophers might make most valuable investigations in Petersburg each in his one line."[188]

To this sort of 'queer and sick world... as in a Russian novel'[189] Nietzsche referred each time he analyzed the nihilism problem.

To make the diagnosis of nihilism means to interpret some symptoms.[190] Usually nihilism is a diagnosis which does not correspond to the patient's opinion about himself and against which he virulently protests. Helmut Thielicke spoke about 'enciphered nihilism' which is different from 'assumed nihilism' when the patient recognizes himself that for him every value has lost its significance, that through value he does not designate anything. Regarding the assumed nihilism, I must underline *the sublime of illness* or 'the masochist sublime'.[191] Nordau was just partially mistaken when he attributed to Nietzsche a sort of sadism-masochism. The sufferance provoked by nihilism can be the source of great creation or, in philosophy, *the only* way to a work of genius. The voluptuousness of sufferance is in this case easy to understand and Nietzsche explains it in *The Gay Science*: "we philosophers, should we become ill, temporarily surrender with body

---

188 Fyodor Dostoievski, *Crimă și pedeapsă*, E.S.P.L.A., București, 1957, p. 424.

189 Friedrich Nietzsche, *Anti-Christ*, p. 603.

190 Helmut Thielicke, *Der Nihilismus. Entstehung, Wesen, Überwindung*, Reichl Verlag, Tübingen, 1950, pp. 40–43.

191 See Aldo Marroni, *L'enigma dell'impuro. La sfida dell'estetico nella società, nella sessualità e nell'arte*, Carocci editore, the chapter *L'enigma del sublime masochistico*, 2007, pp. 143–69.

and soul to the illness – we shut our eyes to ourselves, as it were… permits the question whether it was not illness that inspired the philosopher."[192]

Any physician prescribes a treatment which is meant to slow down the evolution of the disease if this is incurable, or to stop or eliminate the disease. To be capable of prescribing an adequate treatment you must know the nature and the essence of that disease. What is the essence of nihilism? A German author for whom nihilism is a disease phenomenon states that 'the question about the essence of nihilism is similar to that about a very ill person. In the second case the question is: what is the essence of his disease? We could understand nihilism as a sickness (*Erkrankung*) of human essence'.[193] In more precise terminology, we could say that nihilism is a major disease of the human axiological conscience, an illness of his spirit. The physician of culture does all he can in order that the nihilist patient's illness does not escalade or reach its limits.

The transition phases from one system of values to another are nihilist periods. The fall into oblivion of some values brings a shadow of doubt over all values. Any *Umwertung aller Werte* becomes the hypothesis for *Entwertung aller Werte*, an axiological illness named nihilism. 'It's right that people will say about me that I was a *good* physician – not only for me' wrote Nietzsche to his mother.[194] Today the philosopher who lives in a world in which *Umwertung aller Werte* is a phenomenon which can be perceived by anyone, has an extraordinary chance: to be a good physician of culture.

---

192   Friedrich Nietzsche, *The Gay Science*, p. 5.
193   Fritz Leist, *Existenz im Nichts. Versuch einer Analyse des Nihilismus*, Manz Verlag, München, 1961, pp. 45–46.
194   Cf. Ernst Bertram, op. cit., p. 121.

V. The Interpretation of Values

1. Hermeneutic equity

The concept of *Billigkeit* (*equity*), frequently used in the philosophical discourse of the eighteenth century, is a translation of the Greek term *epieikeia*, from Aristotle's *Nicomachean Ethics*, and it generally represents a tempering of the legal provisions in positive law. As well as philosophers, jurists from around the world have always noted the fact that the law rigidly applied turns into its opposite. The strict application of a general law to a particular case often means, not justice, but injustice. *Die Billigkeit* has precisely the role of preventing such a situation, which is so often encountered that Immanuel Kant evoked the following dictum of equity: "the most rigorous right is the greatest injustice".[195] Next, Kant said that "this evil cannot be remedied on the path of right, although it refers to a legal claim, as it belongs only to the *court of conscience* (*Gewissensgericht*)".[196]

Legal or modern philosophical theories have taken from Aristotle the idea that equity is an addition to or correction of positive law, emphasizing that it belongs exclusively to the *court of conscience*, as Kant synthesized these theories of juridical interpretation. It is about the freedom of the interpreter to use it for right or wrong. The intervention of the judge who interprets and applies the law must not be arbitrary, said Aristotle, but must bring to the law the amendment that the legislator would bring if he were present.

In the area of hermeneutics, the term is used somewhat surprisingly by Georg Friedrich Meier in the phrase hermeneutic equity (*hermeneutische Billigkeit*), in the work *Versuch einer allgemeinen Auslegungskunst*, published at Halle in 1757, and this represents the first general hermeneutics in German. If I were allowed to add a subtitle to Meier's book, it would be *Über die hermeneutische Billigkeit*, because *hermeneutic equity* is, in fact, the main object of this book by Georg Friedrich Meier, which is devoted to

---

195   Immanuel Kant, *Die Metaphysik der Sitten*, Verlag von L. Heimann, Berlin, 1870, p. 37.
196   Ibidem.

theoretical and practical aspects of interpretation. Far from being a novelty in its day, *hermeneutische Billigkeit* is nothing but the German transla-tion of the concept of *aequitas hermeneutica*, a commonplace of modern hermeneutics. Before publishing Meier's work *Versuch einer allgemeinen Auslegungskunst*, the principle of hermeneutic equity appeared in the work of Christian Wolff, Johann Heinrich Lambert, Georg Christoph Lichtenberg and a number of other contemporary authors.

Die hermeneutische Billigkeit, as presented in the work of Friedrich Meier, fits naturally into Protestant hermeneutics, where the moral aspects of the process of interpretation are particularly important, as evidenced by the very title of the first of them: *Idea boni interpretis et malitiosi calumniatoris* by Johann Konrad Dannhauer. In the process of interpretation, Flacius Illyricus said, the sources of evil are *error* and *dishonesty*.[197] He insisted on the fact that interpreters often focus on a text in bad faith. It is about those who "although they see, they do not see and although they hear, they do not hear", said Flacius, repeating a passage from the *New Testament* (Matthew, 13.13).[198] Once the abuse interpretation was perceived to be a danger, the limitation or suppression of this phenomenon was attempted. Flacius Illyricus, one of the first prominent representatives of Protestant hermeneutics, drew attention to the work *Clavis scripturae sacrae* on the "barbaric misinterpretation" of the biblical text[199] – misinterpretation arising either from not knowing the languages in which the sacred texts were written, from doctrinaire interests or from other characteristics of the interpreters.

The principle of hermeneutic equity, applied by Friedrich Meier, under the influence of Leibniz, to all signs, including natural ones, is defined as follows: "Hermeneutic equity (aequitas hermeneutica) is the tendency of the interpreter to hold that meaning for hermeneutically true that best com-ports with the flawlessness of the originator of the sign, until the opposite is shown".[200] On this hermeneutical principle, on which a rich literature

---

197 Matthias Flacius, *Über den Erkenntnisgrund der Heiligen Schrift*, übersetzt von Lutz Geldsetzer, Janssen Verlag, Düsseldorf, 1968, p. 77.
198 Ibidem, p. 77.
199 Cf. Wilhelm Dilthey, *Leben Schleiermachers*, in *Gesammelte Schriften*, Band XIV, Verlag Vandenhoeck & Ruprecht, Göttingen, 1966, p. 599.
200 Georg Friedrich Meier, *Versuch einer allgemeinen Auslegungskunst*, Stern-Verlag, Düsseldorf, 1965, p. 20.

exists today, I would like to make a few remarks to support the thesis that Friedrich Nietzsche took the concept of *hermeneutische Billigkeit* almost unchanged from Friedrich Meier.

Firstly, it should be noted that Friedrich Meier, in the spirit of rationalism and Enlightenment, tried to eliminate any suspicion of hermeneutic fraud by establishing new rules of interpretation leading almost mathematically to the *sense* of a system of natural or artificial signs. He spoke of "hermeneutical demonstration". Also, concepts such as "*hermeneutische Wahrheit des Sinnes*", "*logische Demonstration des Sinnes*" or "*hermeneutische Gewißheit des Sinnes*",[201] which Meier frequently used in *Versuch einer allgemeinen Auslegungskunst*, highlight the rationalist character of this hermeneutics. And yet, Friedrich Meier permanently forewarned the reader that hermeneutics, as accurate as it may be, can never be a science, but is a *Kunst*. Hermeneutical demonstration can never be mathematical; this is why a *billig* interpreter should always start by openly recognizing the likely nature of his demonstration. If a certain demonstration is presented as "apodictic", then we are clearly dealing with a *hermeneutische Unbilligkeit*.

Secondly, Friedrich Meier correlates *hermeneutische Billigkeit* with *das Prinzip des Besserverstehens*, which was long believed to be a product of German romanticism, especially of Schleiermacher.[202] An author can be wrongly interpreted, but the sense of his discourse can be forged by what Meier called *Akkommodation*.[203] The *unbillig* interpreter fraudulently introduces a false sense of the author's discourse, thus becoming a butcher of thoughts or a virtual assassin. Destructive ideas, completely foreign to an author's intention, can be assigned to him by a certain *Akkommodation*.

Die hermeneutische Billigkeit is meant to temper the enthusiasm of those who want at all costs to understand an author better than he understood himself. *Das Prinzip des Besserverstehens*, which is also seen in the work of Christian Wolff, of Chladenius and of a number of other authors of modern

---

201 Ibidem, pp. 122–123.
202 Luigi Cataldi Madonna, *Die unzeitgemässe Hermeneutik Christian Wollfs*, in Axel Bühler (Hg.): *Unzeitgemässe Hermeneutik: Verstehen und Interpretation im Denken der Aufklärung*, Vittorio Klostermann, Frankfurt am Main, 1994, p. 35.
203 Georg Friedrich Meier, op. cit., pp. 66–67.

times, is formulated with all clarity by Schleiermacher, who adopted almost exactly the meaning attributed to it by Friedrich Meier: "*Die Aufgabe [der Interpretation] ist auch so ausdrücken, "die Rede zuerst ebensogut und dann besser zu verstehen als ihr Urheber"*".[204] Usually, the first part of this famous hermeneutic principle is ignored, but it is essential to understand how misrepresentation can be avoided and especially to be able to expose the abuses of some *unbillig* interpreters, who act in bad faith and "with hatred for the creator of sings".[205]

Thirdly, hermeneutic inequity can manifest itself not only when *Nebenbegriffe* that are in contradiction with the author's imperfections are assigned to him, but also when they are ignored. An author can also be destroyed when the interpreter refuses to come out of the discourse letter of the author and of the ideas explicitly stated by him. In other words, an author may be sacrificed by assigning to him, through interpretation, too much or too little compared to what the sense of his discourse actually contains, a sense that can be fertile or sterile, as Friedrich Meier said.

Fourthly, under the influence of Leibniz, Friedrich Meier ranked first the problem of hermeneutic equity regarding the interpretation of natural signs. A *billig* interpreter must start from the premise that they were chosen rationally by God and are consistent with the perfection of the creator of the universe. More than any other book, *the book of nature* must be interpreted by strictly complying with the principle of hermeneutic equity. The model of such interpretation is represented by Leibniz's *Theodicy*.

Fifthly, hermeneutische Billigkeit is characterized by the love of the interpreter for the creator of signs.[206] This principle, formulated and applied first to natural signs, is then transposed into the field of artificial signs. An *unbillig* interpreter will consider as true, in terms of hermeneutics, a signifiier that is evidence of the incompleteness of the author of signs, without arguments in this respect. As already noted, under the pretext of a better understanding, an author is often destroyed by an *Akkommodation* or by an abusive interpretation. In such a case, *hermeneutische Unbilligkeit* becomes a form

---

204 F.D.E. Schleiermacher, *Hermeneutik und Kritik*, Suhrkamp Verlag, Frankfurt am Main, 1995, p. 94.
205 Georg Friedrich Meier, op. cit., p. 48.
206 Ibidem, p. 46.

of *Inhumanität*, as characterized by Herder.[207] An *Akkommodation* is not a simple hermeneutic error, but is full of hatred and is a perverse interpretation because the interpreter introduces into the discourse a hermeneutic sense that is false (*ein hermeneutisch falscher Sinn*)[208] but that closely resembles the true sense. In short, an *Akkommodation* is a hermeneutic fraud.

Immanuel Kant used the concept of *Billigkeit* not only in the *Metaphysics of Morals* and other moral-political works, but also in the *General Logic* he was teaching to his students, as is well known, based on Georg Friedrich Meier's work *Vernunftlehre*. Kant's work *The Logic* is the first example of the use of Friedrich Meier's concept of *Billigkeit* in fields other than that of interpretation of signs. Gradually, it would expand to other areas, it would be partly defined and Friedrich Meier would be consigned to oblivion, although the concept of *hermeneutische Billigkeit* was to become increasingly present in the form of psychological interpretation by Schleiermacher, of a *"große Gesetz der Billigkeit"* by Herder, of *Anwendung* by Gadamer, of axiological neutrality by Max Weber, and so on.

It might seem paradoxical, but the philosopher who, in the nineteenth century, preserved in the concept of *Billigkeit* the meaning closest to that attributed to it by Friedrich Meier was Friedrich Nietzsche. Moreover, the way the concept of *Billigkeit* is explained in the *Genealogy of Morals* may represent an explanation of the fact that today *billig* is a term used almost exclusively in a commercial sense. Expressions such as *"ein billiger Preis"* for a certain product or commercial claims such as *"gut und billig"* are well known to the general public today. *Billigkeit* is no longer, in any case, an important topic of philosophical reflection. But Friedrich Nietzsche reproduced very clearly the very close relationship that *Billigkeit* once had with both economic values and moral values, such that he defined man as a "measuring animal".[209] This faculty of man to measure and assess everything is, according to Friedrich Nietzsche, the primary source of any justice or equity, including those in the area of interpretation of texts. He was concerned about *hermeneutic equity*, but he quickly abandoned this

---

207   Johann Gottfried Herder, *Ideen zur Philosophie der Geschichte der Menschheit*, Löwit-Verlag, Wiesbaden, 1966, p. 411.
208   Georg Friedrich Meier, op. cit., p. 66.
209   Friedrich Nietzsche, *On the Genealogy of Morals*, p. 51.

concept because it had no basis in reality. It is more likely that the opposite phenomenon, *hermeneutic inequity*, represents the rule in human history. A *billig* hermeneut is the exception, or a borderline case that has only a purely theoretical role. In the case of a lower dose of hate, *die Billigkeit* suddenly turns into *Unbilligkeit*. The dishonest interpreter is the man of resentment.[210] Moreover, "There is no doubt that on average just a tiny amount of aggression, malice, and insinuation is sufficient to make even the most honest people see red and to deprive them of an impartial eye".[211]

Friedrich Nietzsche, as well as Georg Friedrich Meier, associated *Unbilligkeit* with hatred. When the sentiment of hatred appears "any consideration for *Billigkeit* disappears".[212] In a fragment about *The Natural Value of Egoism*, Nietzsche referred to *Billigkeit* to reward someone who make a gesture that the "worldly justice", in all its forms, condemned it. It is about recognizing the value of selfishness, as long as the egoist is regarded as *"the ascending line of life* ... If he represents descending development, decay, chronic degeneration, sickening, then he can be accorded little value, and elementary fairness (*Billigkeit*) demands that he *takes away* as little as possible from the well-constituted. He is no better than a parasite on them".[213] In other words, it is fair to give way to those in force as much of your resources, as long as you are in vital decline.

This conception of the value of selfishness may seem barbaric and, in any case, bizarre, but it opens up a new perspective on all sublime facts in terms of morality. In the event of a shipwreck, for example, all passengers have an equal right to survival. The selfishness of all must be treated equally by "worldly justice", as having the same value. But such *justice* must be corrected by *equity*. From this perspective, as conceived by Friedrich Nietzsche, the selfishness of the young man who is just starting his life is more justified than that of an old man. This conception of *justice*, *equity* and the *value of selfishness* is not divorced from reality: on the contrary, it is in perfect agreement with those rare human actions that are morally sublime. It is

---

210 Ibidem, p. 55.
211 Ibidem.
212 Friedrich Nietzsche, *Omenesc, prea omenesc*, I, Editura Hestia, Timișoara, 2000, p. 184.
213 Friedrich Nietzsche, *Twilight of the Idols*, p. 97.

known, for instance, that in some cases of shipwreck where the means of rescue on board have been insufficient, some, on their own initiative and in accordance with their own conception of *equity*, have given up their places in the rescue boats to those younger than themselves.

2. Corruption and interpretation

In an excerpt from *The Gay Science* called *The signs of corruption*, Friedrich Nietzsche made the following remark about torturing a person through interpretation, a phenomenon that peaked in the period of decadence of a culture: "I concede that cruelty now *refines* itself ...; wounding and torturing with word and eye reaches its highest cultivation in times of corruption – it is now alone that *malice* and the delight in malice are born. People who live in an age of corruption are witty and slanderous; they know that there are other kinds of murder than by dagger or assault; they also know that whatever is *well said* is believed".[214] From this perspective, the principle of *hermeneutic equity* becomes particularly important because it can serve as a criterion of truth in the area of interpretation. But, for Friedrich Nietzsche, the interpreter is almost always *lacking equity (unbillig)*. In his activity, he is driven by the pettiest interests. The *science of interpretation* does not exist and it cannot ever exist as science. It is a mere invention, a means to torture the reader, so that what it is *well said*, as Friedrich Nietzsche phrased it, will not only be believed, but will also be *demonstrated* through an alleged science of interpretation. A new education of the human race requires a complete and final renunciation of "this execrable manner of Christian interpreting",[215] which is dishonest and always hateful.

"Our values are *introduced* into things through *interpretation*",[216] said Friedrich Nietzsche. For this reason, interpretation is an essential concept of Friedrich Nietzsche's axiology. The problem of the interpretation of values, although present in all his work, is theoretically exposed in the *Third Treatise* of the *Genealogy of Morals*, called *What is the Meaning of Ascetic Ideals?* Friedrich Nietzsche's answer to this question is that it depends on the

---

214 Friedrich Nietzsche, *The Gay Science*, pp. 47–48.
215 Friedrich Nietzsche, *The Dawn of Day*, available at http://www.gutenberg.org/files/39955/39955-h/39955-h.html. Accessed February 28, 2016.
216 Friedrich Nietzsche, *Voința de putere*, Editura Aion, București, 1999, p. 389.

interpreter. He can be honest (*billig*) or dishonest, but there is also another type that is particularly interesting in terms of how values are interpreted. It is that of the *dishonest interpreter* for whom the dishonesty of interpretation becomes second nature: he falsifies reality through interpretation without having fraud on his conscience. Such an interpreter acts with all the naivety that equity personified would. This is, Nietzsche said, the priest who exercises his will to power through a cunning interpretation, but very cleaver of the ascetic ideals.

Before exposing how the priest interprets ascetic ideals, Friedrich Nietzsche referred to artists and philosophers. No one is honest in the interpretations and evaluations of these ideals. For instance, "the artists: for some time now, these artists have lacked sufficient independence in the world and in their stance *towards* the world for their value-judgements and re-evaluations to merit attention *in their own right*! They have always acted as valets to some ethics or philosophy or religion".[217] Friedrich Nietzsche illustrates the artists" intellectual dishonesty with the example of Richard Wagner, who became, for instance, Schopenhaurian when this favoured his own ascent in European culture. Like Wagner, all artists were opportunistic in relation to those who, by the will to power, were setting the criteria for the hierarchy of values.

"What is the meaning of the ascetic ideal for a philosopher?".[218] Are philosophers more honest than artists regarding the interpretation of a system of values? Are they showing *hermeneutic equity* in the evaluations they make? Friedrich Nietzsche's answer to these questions is definitely negative: "Clearly, these philosophers are far from impartial witnesses and judges of the *values* of the ascetic ideal! They are thinking of *themselves* ... They are thinking of what is most indispensable to *them*".[219]

More than pursuing a personal interest in the interpretation process, the priest uses the ascetic ideal as an instrument of the will to power. He cunningly interprets texts, values, events and moods so that the world of degenerates, which he addresses, believes that it and only it represents humanity. Despite his obvious weakness, the degenerate is convinced by the priest that

---

217 Friedrich Nietzsche, *On the Genealogy of Morals*, p. 81.
218 Ibidem, p. 87.
219 Ibidem.

he is the bearer of the highest values. In this world of degenerates, the desire to reach the top of the hierarchy of values is so great that they do not exclude any means to achieve their goal. "What are they really after? To *represent*, at least, justice, love, wisdom, superiority".[220] Therefore, the hermeneutic dishonesty of the priest was the most efficient instrument for forging the hierarchy of values. These degenerates behave as if values are something immoral and must be destroyed in order to return their non-values to their place. This is why they are, Nietzsche said, bloodthirsty and eager to become the executioners for those who would resist their dirty and unseen attack.

The priest is falsely interpreting a state of affairs so that the lowest values look like "value in itself", and those truly higher are lowered to the statut of non-values. In describing the mechanism of this process, Friedrich Nietzsche insisted on the specifics of the dishonest interpretation of the priest. He demonstrated a total innocence, but "make no mistake here: the most distinctive characteristic of modern souls and modern books is not lying, but an ingrained *innocence* in moral deception".[221] Christianity, through its scholars who have dealt with the interpretation of texts and values, is missing a *sense of honesty* (*Sinn für Redlichkeit*), as it is expressed in *The Dawn of Day*. The Christian hermeneuts "follow an explanation so shameless and capricious that a philologist when he hears it is caught between anger and laughter asking himself again and again: Is it possible? Is it honest? Is it even decent?".[222] This lack of honesty in the problem of interpretation is, as Friedrich Nietzsche said, more visible in Protestantism than in Catholicism and, in more subtle and perverse forms, in the entire Christian culture, and throughout its history an incredible distortion of texts can be noticed, attributing to them meanings that are completely removed from the intention of their authors. "All considered however what more can be expected of a religion which in its formative centuries perpetrated an unprecedented philological farce concerning the Old Testament? I refer to that attempt to tear the Old Testament from the hands of the Jews under the pretext that it contained only Christian doctrines and belonged to the Christians as

---

220   Ibidem, p. 101.
221   Ibidem, 115.
222   Friedrich Nietzsche, *The Dawn of Day*, available at http://www.gutenberg.org/files/39955/39955-h/39955-h.html. Accessed February 28, 2016.

the true people of Israel while the Jews had merely taken it for their own without authority. This was followed by a fury of so-called interpretation and falsification which could not under any circumstances have been done with a good conscience".[223]

The most dangerous and harmful performance of religious interpretation is, Nietzsche said, misinterpretation of the feeling of guilt, or what is called, in religious terminology, *sin*. The ascetic ideal, in whose name the priest falsifies everything through interpretation, represents an invincible power. Could he, however, become a free spirit, like Friedrich Nietzsche, in order to end hermeneutic fraud, which stands out best in the interpretation of the ascetic ideals by priests and theologians? His answer is yes only if the human values that were established fraudulently are totally replaced with the values of the superman. Regarding hermeneutic fraud, practised extensively in Christianity, a certain *Billigkeit* of Friedrich Nietzsche must be noticed. In *The Dawn of Day*, he not only condemned such fraud, but in some way tried to justify its need. In other words, he tried to do some justice to the dishonest interpreter, in the sense that it was about a fight between Christianity and very powerful opposing religious doctrines. In a fight with opponents who were themselves unscrupulous, honesty would have been synonymous with suicide. In the early days of Christianity, interpretation was therefore used as a weapon, as a justifiable means by which the aim should have been achieved at any cost. But the dishonesty of the interpretations and evaluations made by the Christian hermeneuts not only relates to the period in which they had to overcome powerful opponents, but also continued after the triumph of Christianity. "All actions may be traced back to evaluations and all evaluations are either one's own or adopted – the latter being by far the more numerous. Why do we adopt them? Through fear i.e. we think it more advisable to pretend that they are our own and so well do we assimilate them that they become second nature to us."[224]

False interpretation and mimetic evaluation are the most subtle forms through which a civilization becomes corrupted and decay.

---

223   Ibidem.
224   Friedrich Nietzsche, *The Dawn of Day*, available at http://www.gutenberg. org/files/39955/39955-h/39955-h.html. Accessed February 28, 2016.

VI. Friedrich Nietzsche as Apostle of Arthur Schopenhauer

1. The Church of Arthur Schopenhauer

When David Strauss said that Schopenhauer was not in his right mind, he was right, just like those contemporaries of Jesus who said of Him, according to the biblical text, that He was out of his mind (Mark 3:21). But Arthur Schopenhauer, like Jesus, is helped by a group of disciples, all of them being "poor in spirit" and dilettante in matters of philosophy, but hard as a rock in their faith to the new 'Teacher'. Arthur Schopenhauer is, above all, a religious individual. His philosophy, as we will try to show throughout this essay, has essentially an eschatological function. This was noted by, among others, Johannes Volkelt, who characterizes Schopenhauer's conception as a "redemptive philosophy" (*Erlösungsphilosophie*).[225] The more profound is the awareness of the fact that the world in which we are living is the worst of all possible worlds, the more powerful is the philosopher's need to save it. Arthur Schopenhauer's theories about art, genius, sanctity, philosophy and the denial of the will to live, said Volkelt, have as their object the means and the ways by which man can be saved from temporality and materiality.[226]

Being a purely religious spirit, Arthur Schopenhauer never intended to found a philosophical school, but a *church*. He never had students, but disciples in the religious sense of the term 'apprentices', like those who followed Jesus, or, as he himself said many times, *apostles* and *evangelists*. I find it odd that, if I'm not mistaken, no one took seriously Arthur Schopenhauer's speech of his relationship as a religious individual with the followers of his philosophy. In this regard, it was all considered irony and self-irony, which is true, with the indication that the serious side of the irony is much more important than the ludic one. When "Strauss then reacts religiously; that is to say, he again begins to belabour Schopenhauer, to abuse him, to speak of absurdities, blasphemies, dissipations, and even to allege that

---

225 Johannes Volkelt, *Arthur Schopenhauer. Seine Persönlichkeit, seine Lehre, sein Glaube*, Frommanns Verlag, Sturttgart, 1901, p. 52.

226 Ibidem.

Schopenhauer could not have been in his right senses",[227] his disciples came to help him with a typical religious zeal, worthy of the new Redeemer. "Among twelve apostles one must always be hard as stone, in order that upon him the new church may be built." Thus spoke Friedrich Nietzsche, the one who, as we shall see, was "the most necessary apostle" of Arthur Schopenhauer. But his church was based on *blind disciples*. "The disciple and apostle who has no eye for the weakness of the teaching, the religion, etc., blinded by the stature of his master and his own piety towards him, for that reason generally has more power than his master. Without blind disciples, no man or his work has ever gained great influence. Sometimes, to promote the triumph of a form of knowledge means only that one weds it to stupidity, so that the weight of the stupidity also forces the triumph of the knowledge."[228]

Let us now deal with these *blind disciples* of Arthur Schopenhauer. From the perspective of the philosophy department, all these fall into the category of the dilettantes, gathered around their master in the late period of his life. Nobody believed in the value of Schopenhauer's work, except himself and a small group of fanatical followers of his bizarre philosophy. After being rejected by editors when he was trying to publish *Parerga und Paralipomena,* he made another approach to Brockhaus, offering for free the manuscript which contained the *Aphorismen zur Lebensweisheit* that would finally make him famous. "If you reject the manuscript this time, too, you commit an error. Because you have nothing to lose, on the contrary, you have much to gain. Believe what you want about me, but I tell you that my writings are the best that this century gave out."[229] Almost in the same terms, he addressed himself a few days later to the editor Dietrich, of Göttingen, but with no success. Arthur Schopenhauer frequently complained to Julius Frauenstädt, his beloved *disciple*, about a certain plot of the professional philosophers; otherwise he could not explain the refusal

227 Friedrich Nietzsche, *Thoughts Out of Season*, The Edinburgh Press, Edinburgh, 1909, p. 43–44.
228 Friedrich Nietzsche, *Human, All Too Human: A Book for Free Spirit*, University of Nebraska Press, Nebraska, 1996, p. 87.
229 Arthur Schopenhauer, *Gesammelte Briefe*, Bouvier Verlag, Bonn, 1987, p. 244.

of the editors to publish his masterpiece. The humiliation of being treated like any debutant, who beats shyly on the door of an editor, strengthened his belief in the value of his manuscript, and, in general, of his work. A sick world rejects in an organic way a brilliant creation. Further still, this fallen world needed a saviour and it was Schopenhauer.

His work created as a new *Gospel*. Thus Friedrich Nietzsche perceived it, and his work *Schopenhauer as Educator* might have very well been entitled *Schopenhauer as Redeemer*. Here's how he describes his first meeting with that seductive *Erlösungsphilosophie* which he is not only inspired by, but which, as the most needed apostle of it, he will spread in his own way, despite being unschooled systematically so far: "I have been describing nothing but the first, almost physiological, impression made upon me by Schopenhauer, the magical emanation of inner force from one plant of Nature to another, that follows the slightest contact. Analysing it, I find that this influence of Schopenhauer has three elements, his honesty, his joy, and his consistency".[230] This image has been regarded, since the advent of the *Schopenhauer as an educator* work, with disbelief, as being a projection of what Nietzsche himself wanted to be: a philosopher, rather than an objective presentation of Arthur Schopenhauer and of his philosophy.[231]

I think that, on the contrary, Friedrich Nietzsche not only understood exactly that it was about a very special conception, whose purpose was not knowledge, but the redemption of the world, but should have, perhaps, taken his thought to its end and said bluntly that it was about *Schopenhauer as Redeemer*. The experience of Friedrich Nietzsche meeting with Schopenhauer's work resembles that of a religious conversion. It is almost that, as with Augustine, a mysterious voice whispers: "*tolle lege, tolle lege*" and, following this, he has the revelation that "His strength rises like a flame m the calm air, straight up, without a tremor or deviation. He finds his way, without our noticing that he has been seeking it: so surely and cleverly and inevitably does he run his course, as if by some law of gravitation. If anyone have felt what it means to find, in our present world of Centaurs and Chimaeras, a single-hearted and unaffected child of nature who moves

---

230   Friedrich Nietzsche, *Thoughts Out of Season*, in: The complete works of Friedrich Nietzsche 5, The Edimburgh Press, Edimburgh, 1909, p. 117.

231   Johannes Volkelt, op. cit., p. 45.

unconstrained on his own road, he will understand my joy and surprise in discovering Schopenhauer: I knew in him the educator and philosopher I had so long desired. Only, however, in his writings: which was a great loss. All the more did I exert myself to see behind the book the living man whose testament it was, and who promised his inheritance to such as could, and would, be more than his readers – his pupils and his sons".[232] This is a subtle way of saying, in fact, that Arthur Schopenhauer is not simply a philosopher, but a 'teacher' within the neo-testamentary meaning of the term (Matthew 23.8), a *redeemer* of a "world of Centaurs and Chimaeras", a true son of the muses in a world of cultural philistines.

Friedrich Nietzsche noted, rightly, that such a philosopher cannot have ordinary readers, but "children and students", meaning disciples, in the religious sense of the term. Let us return now to those "apprentices" on which Arthur Schopenhauer's philosophical church is based, as a community formed by "that charming overflow of the most intimate energy of a natural being over another", by which Nietzsche himself was embraced. One of his most beloved apostles was Julius Frauenstädt, to whom he complained again, in a letter of September 30th, 1850, that he could not find an editor for *Parerga und Paralipomena*. If it would be published, however, "I hardly leave this last work: because the rest is silence!".[233] Not only did Julius Frauenstädt address him as "Mein werther Apostel" or "Mein lieber alter Apostel", but he uses similar formulas in correspondence with all his followers. Both in his correspondence and in the conversations he had with his disciples, religious formulas of address such as "Hochwürdiger Erz-evangelist" and "aktiver Apostel" are common and, often, used without any trace of irony, as in the following excerpt from a letter to August Becker: "Of the four apostles of mine, you are the one who always understands me best. I say it without any flattery (*Ohne alle Schmeichel gesagt*)".[234]

Not only the correspondence but also his philosophical work represents proof of the fact that Arthur Schopenhauer, although he seems to be an atheist, was a deeply religious spirit. In his letter to Julius Frauenstädt, of September 12th, 1852, he announced with ecstatic happiness the advent of a

---

232 Friedrich Nietzsche, *Thoughts Out of Season*, 118.
233 Arthur Schopenhauer, *Gesammelte Briefe*, 248.
234 Ibidem, p. 280.

new follower of his redemptive philosophy: "The new apostle, an emerging evangelist, Kilzer, is truly a brilliant mind".[235] The way in which Schopenhauer reacts when Julius Frauenstädt communicates that he will soon visit a new apostle to Munich is downright amazing: "I really like this visit to the apostle; it has in it something serious and grandiose: where the two meet in my name, I am present between them".[236] Schopenhauer lives his late glory in an almost mystical way, comparing himself, more in jest, half in earnest, with Jesus, present in the midst of those who gather in his name (Matthew 18:20). Even the *glory*, so much desired and so much later gained by the philosopher, has religious connotations. "Your apostolic work" – Schopenhauer writes to Otto Linder on June 9th, 1853 – "has reached a certain height..."[237]; this makes you think of "the highest places" that the New Testament (Luke 2.14) correlates with the *glory* of God.

It would be wrong to understand the *glory* to which Arthur Schopenhauer was aspiring in its current secular sense. It has a religious meaning, and in all the references of the philosopher to his *gloriola* are invoked the apostles and the evangelists.[238] To the one he calls *the mayor apostle* he writes about "a certain Dr Abel or Dr Buddel, I cannot decipher his name, who seems to be an enthusiastic adorer of my philosophy, as a new *apostle*, who wants to even become an evangelist".[239] The philosopher uses the occasion to express his great joy about what he calls "meine Englische Glorifikation".[240] In his turn, August Becker gets repeated thanks from Schopenhauer for "his apostolic zeal".[241]

Today it may seem exaggerated that Arthur Schopenhauer spoke of his disciples as apostles, but if we consider the German version of the Bible made by Martin Luther, we note that the term *disciple* (*Jünger*) is synonymous with *apostle* (*Apostel*) (Matthew, 10.1–2). Therefore, to speak of his disciples as apostles is not so unusual. What is amazing is the fact that its philosophical school has the structure of a new church in which Arthur

---

235   Ibidem, p. 294.
236   Ibidem.
237   Ibidem, p. 312.
238   Ibidem, p. 314.
239   Ibidem, p. 319.
240   Ibidem.
241   Ibidem, p. 325.

Schopenhauer shared his daguerreotypes as icons, in the middle of which he reigned as a pope, and, actually downright incredibly, he promoted and advanced in his function. His jokes and his ironies about his "apprentices" are but masks of a deep spirit, a thirst for glory, but of one who gained enough wisdom in his life to know that *glory* cannot be obtained other than by means of a triumphant church. In this regard, here is an example of a letter to Julius Frauenstädt of August 17th, 1855: "Yesterday I was visited by the district judge (*Kreisrichter*), Voigtel of Magdeburg, who was *converted* by Dorguth, he is only 28 years old, but he is fanatic about his God and his Gospel".[242]

The disciples of this new "Redeemer" must proselytize. Arthur Schopenhauer's philosophical Church was a missionary one. His teachings had to be spread throughout the world, because the world itself was to be saved and would be saved by this *Erlösungsphilosophie*. "The moral consequences of Christianity to the most extreme asceticism are present with me, but based on the reason and the connection of things; while in Christianity they are supported by mere fables. The belief in these is daily waning; people will, therefore, be forced to turn to my philosophy."[243]

In a letter dated September 7th, 1855, the philosopher of pessimism showed, paradoxically, that he was overjoyed at being visited by various proselytes, each of whom "eagerly studied my works"[244], and that his portrait, which was in the exhibition for about two weeks, was admired by many people. To Carl Grimm he wrote that he received three lithographs of his portrait that were distributed as follows: "One I keep for myself and the two others I sent to Berlin to the two old evangelists (*Urevangelisten*). Because you are now advanced from simple apostle to evangelist, I would send one to you, too if I had more".[245] All these apostles and evangelists of Arthur Schopenhauer prepared, with a quasi-religious enthusiasm, a number of publications about Arthur Schopenhauer, reviews, and translations of

---

242 Ibidem, p. 372.
243 Arthur Schopenhauer, *Some observations of my own philosophy*, in: The Wisdom of Life and other Essays, M. Walter Dunne Washington & London, 1901, p. 233.
244 Arthur Schopenhauer, *Gesammelte Briefe*, 372.
245 Ibidem, 388.

the "true philosophy". Disciples were willing to make any sacrifice for the triumph of the redeeming teaching of their master. One of them, Wilhelm Gewinner, said that Schopenhauer put the accent on the fact that his writings were met with such enthusiasm just by the dilettantes.[246] Only they can be apostles and evangelists for a reason exhibited most clearly in an excerpt from *Parerga und Paralipomena:* they were opposed to the Philistines' culture because their entire apostolic activity was not conducted for money or for any other help, but only for love and for their pleasure.[247]. In this respect, says Schopenhauer, Goethe was also a dilettante in the *Theory of Colours.*[248]

But mostly he enjoyed receiving new evidence that his teaching was apparently completely irreligious: "it appeared as a religion and as a source of inner peace, filling the empty place of the lost faith".[249] Such testimony is a perfect illustration of the thesis that they argue in this essay: Arthur Schopenhauer created a philosophy like a religion, in whose name a small circle of enthusiastic disciples built or at least tried to build a church. "Schopenhauer's philosophy comes from the heart".[250] If it were not so, it would not have spread as if it were a religious doctrine. Its disciples were convinced that such a conception "opens a new era in the history of philosophy".[251]

There are numerous such pieces of evidence attesting to the fact that, when Arthur Schopenhauer spoke of his disciples as apostles and evangelists, he was considering the quasi-religious character of his philosophy. Sometimes he talked in the most serious tone about his philosophical "school", which was constituted by the end of his life, as his "parish" (*Gemeinde*). Schopenhauer writes to Julius Frauenstädt that a new apostle passing through Dresden talked with Bähr about his philosophy. "He belongs to my parishioners from Zürich; all these apostles are known to you."[252] Another apostle from Zürich, Ritter, went to Frankfurt am Main as to a place

---

246 Wilhelm Gewinner, *Arthur Schopenhauer aus persönlichen Umgange dargestellt*, Brockhaus, Leipzig, 1922, p. 199.
247 Arthur Schopenhauer, *Über Gelehrsamkeit und Gelehrte*, in: Parerga und Paralipomena, II, Haffmans Verlag, Zürich, 1991, p. 426–427.
248 Ibidem, p. 427.
249 Wilhelm Gewinner, op. cit., p., 199.
250 Ibidem, p. 163.
251 Ibidem, p. 170.
252 Arthur Schopenhauer, *Gesammelte Briefe*, 389.

of pilgrimage and, on his departure, he kissed the hand of the philosopher as one of a pope, "a ceremony that I cannot get used to"[253], Schopenhauer said, without being able to hide his immense satisfaction at the significance of such a gesture.

Like Christianity, Schopenhauer's philosophy was long kept in the dark; the disciples were forced to retreat somewhat in a kind of cultural catacomb from where they prepared its triumph. "My philosophy" – said Schopenhauer – "was shut out from air and light that no one might see me, and that my natural claims might not be recognized."[254] *Schopenhauer in Vincoli!*: this is the image that the philosopher projected in the mind of his followers. "Thank you for your continued participation in my philosophy and for your apostolic activity for spreading it"[255], Schopenhauer wrote to Julius Bahnsen on December 22nd, 1856; a year later he wrote in almost the same religious language to G.W. Körber: "With these, be welcomed as a new apostle of my teaching".[256] The fact should be noted that Schopenhauer did not use the term *Apostel* for the disciples only in correspondence and in private discussions, but also in his work. For example, he refers to the Reinhold philosopher as "the first apostle of Kant"[257]. Could another philosopher, besides Schopenhauer, also have *apostles and evangelists?* Schopenhauer's answer was, as we have already seen, a positive one, illustrated by Immanuel Kant because he "could yet live both by and for philosophy dependent on the rare circumstance that, for the first time since Divus Antoninus and Divus Julianus, a philosopher sat on the throne. Only under such auspices could the *Critique of Pure Reason* have seen the light".[258]

2. *The aura* of Arthur Schopenhauer

A certain aura, specific to the representations of the saints, was radiating from the image of Schopenhauer, as he is described not only by his devoted

---

253 Ibidem, p. 390.
254 Arthur Schopenhauer, *Über meine eigene Philosophie*, p. 137.
255 Arthur Schopenhauer, *Gesammelte Briefe*, 408.
256 Ibidem, 419.
257 Arthur Schopenhauer, *Über die Universitätsphilosophie*, 171.
258 Arthur Schopenhauer, *The World As Will And Idea* II, trans. R. B. Haldane and J. Kemp, Kegan Paul, Trench, Trübner & Co., London, 1909, p. 354.

disciples, but also by other trustworthy people who knew him closely. If we gathered in one book all these stories about the 'aura' of Schopenhauer, it might become a strange hagiography. It should be noted, however, that this 'aura' is not just a fantasy creation of some enthusiastic followers, neither a mental vision of some fools for the new Redeemer, as those fools were for Jesus, nor a simple retouching of the philosopher's image, as happens in any philosophical schools. Beyond all fantasies and follies which are undoubtedly in the stories by the apostles and evangelists of the almost unearthly personality of their master, the nature of the 'aura' of Schopenhauer is in the meaning given to that term by Walter Benjamin. It's about that enigmatic aura that surrounded the man of genius, unique and unrepeatable, unlike "the common mortal, that manufacture of Nature which she produces by the thousand every day".[259]

When the philosopher was still young, only 29 years old, an Italian came to him and said in all seriousness that on his face he observed something great. As reported by Wilhelm Gewinner, he said: "Signore, Lei deve avere fatto qualche grande opera: non so cosa (sic!) sia, ma lo vedo al suo vis".[260] Also, an Englishman who saw Arthur Schopenhauer for the first time said that he had to be an extraordinary spirit, being amazed by the *aura* of the philosopher. In turn, a Frenchman, also unknown to Schopenhauer, added: "I would like to know what he thinks about us, the others. We must appear very small in his eyes, because he is a superior being".[261] Another Englishman, when was in the same place as Schopenhauer, and when he was asked to change his place, said: "No, I'll sit here, I like to see his intellectual face!".[262] Such magical gatherings often took place, says Wilhelm Gewinner, because Schopenhauer's face radiated a special spirit.

Research into the veracity of these statements is meaningless: it is important that they are reported by one of his apostles, and they are symptomatic of how the philosopher was seen by his disciples. Like in any other religion in this *Erlösungsphilosophie*, the 'truth' of a statement is a matter of faith,

---

259 Arthur Schopenhauer, *The World As Will And Idea*, vol. I., 249.
260 Wilhelm Gewinner, *Arthur Schopenhauer aus persönlichen Umgange dargestellt*, p. 86.
261 Ibidem.
262 Ibidem.

not science. Arthur Schopenhauer's disciples saw in him a chosen character, a superior being, a messenger from heaven to save the worst of all possible worlds. Moreover, their image of their master is similar to that which Schopenhauer himself had of genius, to which an aura was assigned, like saints in the paintings of Raphael and Corregio: "the expression of genius which constitutes the evident family likeness of all highly gifted men consists in this, that in it we distinctly read the liberation, the manumission of the intellect from the service of the will, the predominance of knowledge over volition; and because all anxiety proceeds from the will, and knowledge, on the contrary, is in and for itself painless and serene, this gives to their lofty brow and clear, perceiving glance, which are not subject to the service of the will and its wants, that look of great, almost supernatural serenity which at times breaks through, and consists very well with the melancholy of their other features, especially the mouth, and which in this relation may be aptly described by the motto of Giordano Bruno: In tristitia hilaris, in hilaritate tristis".[263]

Half in jest, half in earnest, the philosopher evokes the 'fanaticism' of some of his disciples, but which he actually enjoys, and that feeds it in a subtle way. Without a certain fanaticism by his first followers, like any other religion, it could never have prevailed. When C. F. Wiesike communicates to Arthur Schopenhauer that he purchased his portrait and that he intends to build him a special room, Schopenhauer replied in a memorable way: "My first chapel!".[264] This is yet another proof that, partially consciously, partly unconsciously, he pursued the establishing of a philosophy as a religion and a philosophical school similar to a church. That statement may seem inappropriate, especially since the literature does not record it other than in anecdotal episodes from the life of Schopenhauer such as those mentioned above. He is, however, a philosopher who undertook honestly the proselytizing that was actually practised in any other philosophical school. "Any philosophy finds its followers. Only the history of philosophy is limited to simple connoisseurs."[265]

---

263   Arthur Schopenhauer, *The World As Will And Idea*, vol. III., 142–143.

264   Wilhelm Gewinner, *Arthur Schopenhauer aus persönlichen Umgange dargestellt*, p. 88.

265   Alexander Riel, *Zum 200. Geburtstag Arthur Schopenhauers. Briefe im Interesse seiner Philosophie*, Verlag Besold, München, 1988, p. 54.

3. Schopenhauer as Redeemer

We now return, more broadly, to the idea that the work of Friedrich Nietzsche, *Schopenhauer as Educator*, mightwell have been entitled *Schopenhauer as Teacher*, in the sense that Jesus was named in this way by his disciples, or, better, *Schopenhauer as Redeemer*. Nietzsche's thesis is quite clear: Arthur Schopenhauer, a very special character, unique in his time, was meant to heal a sick, decadent and degenerate world. How should German culture actually be? So that, says Nietzsche, it should be proper to Arthur Schopenhauer, "their only philosopher in this century ... Here you have the philosopher – now search for Culture proper to him. And if you are able to divine what kind of culture that would have to be, which would correspond to such a philosopher, then you have in this divination, already *passed sentence* on all your culture and on yourselves".[266]

The miraculous effects of the meeting of some readers with Schopenhauer's work should not be viewed solely through the prism of irony or an anecdote. There is evidence from reliable persons, both regarding the *aura* of the philosopher and the fabulous therapeutic effect that his works had on some readers. Arthur Schopenhauer wrote to Frauenstädt on September 23rd, 1853: "Two weeks ago some Dr Kriegskotte came to me, a middle school teacher ..., a grown man, about 40 years, came, looked at me and fear seized me when he cried: I want to see you! I'm coming to see you! He showed great enthusiasm. My philosophy would have given back the life. *Charmant*!".[267] Indeed, the pessimism that instills optimism and trust in life can only be *charmant*! As usual, he did not then use irony other than as a mask to express the truths so strange that even he could not afford to tell them directly. But he had no doubt that he would be 'canonized' like saints as soon as he died, or that his philosophy had not only therapeutic powers, but soteriological ones. The philosophy of denial of the will to live would redeem the world. Such a belief is expressed by him in a veiled way, not

---

266 Friedrich Nietzsche, *The Relation of Schopenhauer's Philosophy to a German Culture: Preface to an Unwritten Book*, trans. Maximilian A. Mügge, in: The complete works of Friedrich Nietzsche, The Macmillan Company, New York, 1911, p. 69.
267 Arthur Schopenhauer, *Gesammelte Briefe*, 328.

just in front of his 'disciple', but also before people outside of his 'church', who visited him and met him by chance in Frankfurt am Main.

The extinction in Nirvana is the redemption promised by Schopenhauer to his disciples. P. Challemel-Lacour, one of his first French disciples, stated that "the doctrine of Schopenhauer aims, first of all, at the search for truth, in fact, it has great practical ambitions, liking it to join, by moral conclusions, to Christianity and the holy religion of Buddhism. Explaining the world, it gives the law of redemption".[268] The same French disciple, as well as everyone else, said that Schopenhauer sometimes spoke like a priest or pastor, and it was hard not to get seduced by the demonic spell of his speeches. Almost all his disciples always evoked him with a typical religious thrill, as P. Challemel-Lacour did, after he met him in Frankfurt: "Every time I remember his words, a thrill that I well know, crosses head to toe, as an icy blast would leave the half-closed door of the nothingness. As he spoke, I thought of that *farewell* ... of Leopardi... I understood then that the most audacious poet would not be able to touch the supreme tarbenacle and the hand of a philosopher is needed to commit certain profanities".[269] Arthur Schopenhauer is one from whom Friedrich Nietzsche learned "how to philosophize with the hammer", as idols were shattered, all values were flipped.

Friedrich Nietzsche expressed more clearly what all the other apostles and evangelists, less trained in philosophy, described as extraordinary in their meeting with Arthur Schopenhauer, the repulsive pessimist old man who nonetheless immediately seduced them with his aura of a prophet: he was a new *Redeemer*. His mission was to save the culture of the world from the greedy hands of Philistines and to open a new era in human history. A culture in which Arthur Schopenhauer does not find his place is a sick culture, philistinism being the cancer that grinds it irreparably. Who are these *Philistines* in the sense of Friedrich Nietzsche? There are those profiteers of culture that dominate it with that cunning specific to the natures of low character, as Friedrich Nietzsche specifies. "As everyone knows, the word 'Philistine' is borrowed from the vernacular of student-life, and, in its widest and most

---

268 P. Challemel-Lacour, "Un bouddhiste contemporain en Allemagne: Arthur Schopenhauer", Revue des deux mondes (Mars, 1870), p. 331.

269 P. Challemel-Lacour, *Études et réflexions d'un pessimiste*, Charpentier, Paris, 1901, p. 68–69.

popular sense, it signifies the reverse of a son of the Muses, of an artist, and of the genuine man of culture."[270] As the whole of society is decadent, it is no wonder that he thinks that he is the measure of all things and he sets himself up as the "son of the muses". In a world dominated by philistines of culture, a genuine philosopher, like Schopenhauer, could not end otherwise than crucified and not without basis did he complain to the disciples that he was forced to carry his cross, whose burden he fully felt. "The Culture-Philistine either does no more than ward off the blows, or else he denies, holds his tongue, stops his ears, and refuses to face facts... Nobody, however, is more disliked by him than the man who regards him as a Philistine, and tells him what he is--namely, the barrier in the way of all powerful men and creators, the labyrinth for all who doubt and go astray, the swamp for all the weak and the weary, the fetters of those who would run towards lofty goals, the poisonous mist that chokes all germinating hopes, the scorching sand to all those German thinkers who seek for, and thirst after, a new life."[271] It is understood that in a Philistine civilization, Arthur Schopenhauer appears as an idealist who must not be taken seriously; more, he must be annihilated by defamation, by abusive interpretation of his work or, more simply and effectively, through a conspiracy of silence.

What to do to survive with dignity in an undignified world? "*To be or not to be*, that is the question he has asked himself...Through his work he answered it."[272] In short, the answer of Arthur Schopenhauer to the Hamletian question is: to be *as if* you did not exist. This *als ob* of Kantian philosophy is that which directs all philosophical reflections, especially the ethical ones.

The philosophy of denial of the will to live includes the saving knowledge that occurs suddenly, like a revelation. The work of Arthur Schopenhauer is only an *initiation* into an almost *mystical* sense of this knowledge that suppresses the will to live. Moreover, the last part of *The World as Will and Representation* is a true *Apocalypse*.

---

270   Friedrich Nietzsche, *Thoughts Out of Season*, 11.

271   Ibidem, 13.

272   Karl Pisa, *Schopenhauer. Kronzeuge einer unheilen Welt*, Paul Neff Verlag, Berlin, 1977, p. 389.

"The will to live can only destroy its manifestation at this place and time. It itself can never be transcended except through knowledge. Thus the only way of salvation is, that the will shall manifest itself unrestrictedly, in order that in this individual manifestation it may come to apprehend its own nature. Only as the result of this knowledge can the will transcend itself, and thereby end the suffering which is inseparable from its manifestation. It is quite impossible to accomplish this end by physical force, as by destroying the germ, or by killing the new-born child, or by committing suicide."[273] Although, long before Schopenhauer, there were a number of saints and ascetics who denied the will to live, as he himself says, however, the world whose redemption the philosopher still thinks about has not disappeared. The *redemptive philosophy* is, in essence, a consolation before death. The wise man must settle accounts with life in a convenient way. You must behave before death *as if* the entire universe would die together with you. It is understood that in such a situation the *serenity* about which Schopenhauer speaks, and which he admirably illustrates with certain saints and ascetics, includes naturally the face of the dying. What is there to regret if everything happens *as if*, atonce with your disappearance, the world itself disappears? This thought is the "*quieter*" evoked by Arthur Schopenhauer in his "Apocalypse".[274] He becomes, thus, the new Redeemer, who, unlike the old one, seems to say: "I am the way, the truth and the *Nothingness*".

The philosophy of Arthur Schopenhauer is a practical one and the knowledge nothing but the appropriate means to achieve the purpose to which the great initiates aspired: redemption of the man and the world. His conception becomes thus a *saving philosophy* (*Erlösungsphilosophie*), as characterized by Wilhelm Gewinner and the other disciples.

From this perspective, Arthur Schopenhauer created a philosophy similar to a religion, meant to take the place of Christianity, which was in decline, and a philosophical school similar to a church, in which its disciples were called, rightly, apostles and evangelists.

---

273 Arthur Schopenhauer, *The World As Will And Idea*, vol. I., 512.
274 Ibidem, 515.

VII. Nietzsche's Tyranny of Values

1. *The new passion*

The thesis I defend and argue for below can be briefly formulated as follows: the phenomenon known in axiology as the *tyranny of values* is powerfully manifested by Friedrich Nietzsche; however, it is not about a certain theorization of it, but the fact that a certain value becomes in its spirit somewhat "absolute".

We use here the concept of *tyranny of values*, as defined by Nicolai Hartmann in his famous work *Ethics*: "Every value – when once it has garnered power over a person – has the tendency to set itself up as sole tyrant of the whole human ethos, and indeed at the expense of other values, even of such as are not inherently opposed to it ... It is the tendency to crowd out other values from the range of emotional appraisement. Such tyranny shows itself plainly in the one-sided types of current morality, in the well-known intolerance of man ... towards the customs of foreigners, but still more in the individual person's obsession by one single value. Thus there exists a fanaticism of justice *(fiat justitia pereat mundus)*".[275]

In metaphorical language and in his unmistakable style, Friedrich Nietzsche addressed to some extent all the major themes of axiology, a discipline that would later become the science of values and to whose appearance his work made an exceptional contribution. He spoke from his own experience about the tyranny of values, as a *man of resentment*. The dominant value of Friedrich Nietzsche's spirit is *honesty (Redlichkeit)*. This *Redlichkeit*, which is difficult to translate precisely, is the main feature of what he calls *free spirit*. Starting with *Beyond Good and Evil*, a paper published in 1886, Nietzsche designated his ideal of a philosopher by the expression *der freie Geist*. A philosopher without intellectual and moral honesty would be inconceivable, but only a *free spirit* can be honest. But the *tyranny of values* affects even the axiological conscience of a *free spirit*. In other words, freedom, like any other value, tends to be tyrannical. When

---

275 Nicolai Hartmann, *Ethics*, vol. II, Allen & Macmillan Company, London/ New York, 1932, p. 423.

it is exercised in excess, it turns into its opposite. From a value, it becomes a non-value, or, as Nietzsche said, "Every virtue inclines to stupidity".[276] The *free spirit* eventually becomes the *slave* of its own excessive liberty. Friedrich Nietzsche, who became a free spirit, as he said himself countless times, lived the experience of this danger in a dramatic manner. This is how he described it in *Beyond Good and Evil*: "The *pia fraus* is still more repugnant to the taste (the "piety") of the free spirit (the "pious man of knowledge") than the *impia fraus*. Hence the profound lack of judgment, in comparison with the Church, characteristic of the type "free spirit" – as *its* non-freedom".[277] When *honesty*, which is the central value of the free spirit, becomes tyrannical, it transforms into its opposite, into an unfree spirit, like a demon possessed. This is a paradox that Friedrich Nietzsche fully felt and expressed in different forms. "Honesty, granting that it is the virtue of which we cannot rid ourselves, we free spirits – well, we will labour at it with all our perversity and love, and not tire of "perfecting" ourselves in our virtue, which alone remains".[278] This *Redlichkeit* became for Friedrich Nietzsche an authentic obsession. He realized the danger represented by a value, in this case honesty, taken to extremes, but for this very reason he was not willing to make any compromise. His slogan was not: let honesty triumph so that the human world perishes along with its entire tablet of forged values. He spoke about "a kind of cruelty of the intellectual conscience and taste, which every courageous thinker will acknowledge in himself".[279] Free or even very free spirits, as Friedrich Nietzsche pointed out, have a kind of "extravagant honesty". However, *Redlichkeit* would remain for him the value over which he was not willing to make any compromise. In a superb essay dedicated to Friedrich Nietzsche, Stefan Zweig said "Passio nuova or the new passion, this is what a book planned by the early Nietzsche was to be called. He never wrote it, but – more than that – he lived it. Because passionate sincerity, fanatic gladness, excessive love of truth taken to the point of torture are the root generating Nietzsche's

---

276 Friedrich Nietzsche, *Beyond Good and Evil*, available at https://www.guten-berg.org/ebooks/4363. Accessed February 28, 2016.
277 Ibidem.
278 Ibidem.
279 Ibidem.

growth and evolution".[280] Even if he did not manage to write the book mentioned by Stefan Zweig, he nonetheless wrote a short fragment about the new passion. It is about the passion for knowledge whose essence is precisely the intellectual and moral honesty of the researcher. "Knowledge within us has developed into a passion, which does not shrink from any sacrifice, and at bottom fears nothing but its own extinction. We sincerely believe that all humanity, weighed down as it is by the burden of this passion, are bound to feel more exalted and comforted than formerly, when they had not yet overcome the longing for the coarser satisfaction which accompanies barbarism. It may be that mankind may perish eventually from this passion for knowledge".[281]

In *The Antichrist*, *honesty*, as a value that has demonically possessed Friedrich Nietzsche's soul, apocalyptically destroys all other values. They are unmasked as the means most treacherous of the general corruption of humanity, and Friedrich Nietzsche becomes the implacable fanatic of the fight against this colossal *Korruption*. His slogan in this fight to the death for *Umwertung aller Werte* is poetically expressed in *The Gay Science*: "One law applies to you: be thine!".[282]

It is somewhat surprising that Friedrich Nietzsche illustrated his ideas on the moral purity and intellectual honesty that characterize the "free spirit" specifically with the personality of Jesus. "One could, with some freedom of expression, call Jesus a "free spirit" – he cares nothing for what is fixed: the word *killeth*, everything fixed *killeth*. The concept, the *experience* "life" in the only form he knows it is opposed to any kind of word, formula, law, faith, dogma. He speaks only of the inmost thing ..., everything else, the whole of reality, the whole of nature, language itself, possesses for him merely the value of a sign, a metaphor".[283]

The values taught by Jesus were, said Nietzsche, very quickly forged by priests and theologians lacking *Redlichkeit*. Only a spirit that became

280   Stefan Zweig, *Tolstoi. Nietzsche*, Editura ştiinţifică, Bucureşti, 1996, p. 190.
281   Friedrich Nietzsche, *The Dawn of Day*, available at http://www.gutenberg. org/files/39955/39955-h/39955-h.html. Accessed February 28, 2016.
282   Friedrich Nietzsche, *The Gay Science*, Cambridge University Press, 2009, p. 23.
283   Friedrich Nietzsche, *The Antichrist*, Penguin Books, 2003, pp. 156–157.

free, such as Friedrich Nietzsche, could truly understand the essence of the original Christianity, as shown in the *Antichrist*. Moreover, this understanding was so profound that he identified himself with Jesus and, not coincidentally, would look from then on like the *Crucified*. On his last day of lucidity and the first day of his insanity, Nietzsche seemed to say that he was the second authentic Christian, after the first had been killed by those who plundered and forged his teaching. The saving philosophy of Jesus, so valued in the *Antichrist*, was transformed by the crafty artisans, led by Paul, into a gruesome prison of the mind and man's soul. Friedrich Nietzsche became a *free spirit* and, in this capacity, he was also the *dynamite* blowing up this horrible prison of the mind, from which he, the fearless knight of knowledge, managed to escape, thus becoming the new saviour.

2. Nietzsche, the death and the devil

As is well known, Friedrich Nietzsche did not have a special aptitude for towards painting. He seldom illustrated his ideas about values with works by painters, except for Claude Laurrain. But there is one other exception. It concerns a painting that really obsessed him and to which we have to refer in order to clarify some aspects of Friedrich Nietzsche's axiology, which are, at first glance, either enigmatic, or unacceptable in terms of morality. It is Albrecht Dürer's famous work *Knight, Death and the Devil*. This work is evoked in *The Birth of Tragedy* when the German culture is presented as exhausted, but with the potential to be reborn by strong personalities, whose model could be Dürer's knight. "A cheerless solitary wanderer could choose for himself no better symbol than the Knight with Death and the Devil, as Dürer has sketched him for us, the mail-clad knight, grim and stern of visage, who is able, unperturbed by his gruesome companions, and yet hopelessly, to pursue his terrible path with horse and hound alone."[284]

Even though the author of *The Birth of Tragedy* was later brutally separated from Schopenhauer, Dürer's drawing continued to preoccupy him, only this time the knight in this terrible company is none other than Friedrich

---

284 Friedrich Nietzsche, *The Birth of Tragedy*, available at http://www.gutenberg. org/files/51356/51356-h/51356-h.htm. Accessed February 28, 2016.

Nietzsche. It was he who followed his goal so that, in *Ecce Homo*, he would be able to affirm that it was destiny (*ein Schicksal*). What we are interested in here from Dürer's famous work is the devil. My thesis on Nietzsche's passion for this work, formulated in a very general way, is as follows: nothing great can be achieved in the world without the intervention of the devil. The devil, as a symbol of evil and non-value, is present in any creative process. For Friedrich Nietzsche, no creation is possible without destruction; no exaltation of the human spirit to the light is possible without it being deepened in the dark. Nietzsche's thesis about *creating wickedness*, poetically exposed in *Thus Spoke Zarathustra*, is reused in rigorous terms in *Ecce Homo* and applied to his own personality: "I am by far the most terrible human being there has ever been; this does not mean I shall not be the most beneficent. I know joy in destruction to a degree corresponding to my strength for destruction – in both I obey my Dionysian nature, which does not know how to separate No-doing from Yes-saying. I am the first immoralist: I am therewith the destroyer par excellence".[285]

In *The Genealogy of Morals*, Schopenhauer is again considered an authentic philosopher, "a man and knight with an iron gaze, who has the courage to be himself".[286] In terms less metaphorical than in *The Birth of Tragedy*, Nietzsche exposed here, once again, his own interpretation of Dürer's parable: the knight accompanied by death and the devil is the knight of truth at any cost, no matter how inconvenient or dangerous this truth would be.

Where does the impulse of the knight of knowledge to confront any danger to get to the truth come from? Where does the motivation of the foolhardy creator come from, and who, to impose his own creations, is willing to fight and to reverse all values presented to him? The answer to these questions, for Nietzsche, is just one: from the devil. Metaphorically speaking, without being constantly "tortured" by the devil, the creator would soften very quickly. Without an *instrumentum diaboli*, Nietzsche said, neither Schopenhauer nor any other creator could ever achieve anything magnificent. Therefore, the devil keeps the knight of knowledge and creation on form, while death

---

285 Friedrich Nietzsche, *Ecce Homo*, available at https://archive.org/details/TheCompleteWorksOfFriedrichNietzschevol.17-EcceHomo. Accessed February 28, 2016.

286 Friedrich Nietzsche, *On the Genealogy of Morals*, p. 82.

reminds him constantly that the time available for achieving higher goals is very limited so he needs to hurry. The fact that Nietzsche often characterized himself as a warrior is further proof that Dürer's work *Knight, Death and the Devil* was haunting him. The "knight" Friedrich Nietzsche's deep need of the "devil" is expressed in *Ecce Homo* as follows: "I am by nature warlike. To attack is among my instincts. To be able to be an enemy, to be an enemy – that perhaps presupposes a strong nature, it is in any event a condition of every strong nature. It needs resistances, consequently it seeks resistances: the aggressive pathos belongs as necessarily to strength as the feeling of vengefulness and vindictiveness does to weakness".[287]

The chivalrous courage of the truth is necessary precisely because the great truths are dangerous. They are not for the weak or for cowards, as stated in *Beyond Good and Evil*: "A thing could be *true*, although it were in the highest degree injurious and dangerous; indeed, the fundamental constitution of existence might be such that one succumbed by a full knowledge of it – so that the strength of a mind might be measured by the amount of "truth" it could endure – or to speak more plainly, by the extent to which it *required* truth attenuated, veiled, sweetened, damped, and falsified".[288]

The fact that Friedrich Nietzsche presented himself as a *knight of truth* who, from the perspective of a creator, was happy to be in the company of the devil, aroused horror among those who noticed this association. Since the late nineteenth century, works about Nietzsche have appeared which state that he embodied the power of evil. His philosophy is crossed by a satanic breath. Nietzsche is not just the author of the *Antichrist*, but the *antichrist* himself.[289] But such interpretations of his philosophies are based on a misunderstanding. The image of Friedrich Nietzsche as a dangerous thinker is well known today, but he is only a *knight of truth*.

287　Friedrich Nietzsche, *Ecce Homo*, available at https://archive.org/details/TheCompleteWorksOfFriedrichNietzschevol.17-EcceHomo. Accessed February 28, 2016.

288　Friedrich Nietzsche, *Beyond Good and Evil*, available at https://www.gutenberg.org/ebooks/4363. Accessed February 28, 2016.

289　Peter Köster, *Der verbotene Philosoph: Studien zu den Anfängen der katholischen Nietzsche-Rezeption in Deutschland (1890–1918)*, Walter de Gruyter, Berlin, 1998, p. 44.

Regarding Friedrich Nietzsche's courage to tell the whole truth, it should be noted that it was perceived more as *crazy* than as *chivalrous*. For example, he would forcibly express that the *will to power* was the criterion of truth, that the strong always determine what is good and what is bad. Was it not said, rightly, that history is always written by the victors? The value judgements of the victors, not those of the losers, have always been considered valid. After all, this idea is a banal truth that everyone accepts in silence or delivers in a whisper. Only an "insane" man like Friedrich Nietzsche had the courage to shout it loudly in the public square. In fact, the ideas of his that contributed to his extraordinary success in European culture are truths that it requires a lot of courage to utter aloud. The public finds in Friedrich Nietzsche's book truths that he sensed but which he refused to express because of cowardice. "Three-quarters of all the evil committed in the world is due to timidity; and this is above all a physiological process!".[290]

Dürer's work *Knight, Death and the Devil* contains a terrible truth, but one attenuated by its allegorical form. However, Nietzsche assumed the risk of speaking this terrible truth without censorship: nothing can be achieved without the devil, in the sense that without some *fraus* no noble goal could be achieved and no masterpiece could be created. Nietzsche invoked Napoleon, "this synthesis of the *inhuman* and the *superman*",[291] as an example of this inconvenient truth. All that mankind has that is valuable, said Nietzsche, was acquired through crime. Without the "devil" and without death no man would ever have tried to perpetuate himself through a masterpiece. The role of companion of the knight of knowledge and creation played by the "devil" is emphasized in *Beyond Good and Evil* as follows: "The devil has the most extensive perspectives for God; on that account he keeps so far away from him: – the devil, in effect, as the oldest friend of knowledge".[292]

---

290   Friedrich Nietzsche, *The Dawn of Day*, available at http://www.gutenberg.org/files/39955/39955-h/39955-h.html. Accessed February 28, 2016.
291   Friedrich Nietzsche, *On the Genealogy of Morals*, p. 36.
292   Friedrich Nietzsche, *Beyond Good and Evil*, available at https://www.gutenberg.org/ebooks/4363. Accessed February 28, 2016.

3. The demonism of power

The role of the "devil" in creation can be highlighted most easily in the field of politics. Napoleon, as an artist of political power, represented, for Friedrich Nietzsche, the embodiment of the will to power. He acted outside morality and determined on his own the new axiological order. "The strongest and most evil spirits have so far done the most to advance humanity ... Mostly by force of arms, by toppling boundary stones, by violating pieties – but also by means of new religions and moralities! In every teacher and preacher of what is new we find the same "mischief" that makes conquerors infamous ... What is *new*, however, is under all circumstances *evil*, being that which wants to conquer, to overthrow the old boundary stones and pieties".[293] The demonism of power is what fascinated Friedrich Nietzsche in Napoleon, as a Renaissance man who saw something like a personal enemy in modern ideas and civilization generally.[294] Napoleon was a *free spirit*, which is the same thing as a *strong man* in Nietzsche's language, who was prepared to put *evil* to work to achieve his goals. Through their *bad* side, individuals and communities are not only active but can also become creative. Let us consider how Friedrich Nietzsche spoke on behalf of all free spirits, of whom Napoleon was one: "Let us go with all our "devils" to the help of our "God"! It is probable that people will misunderstand and mistake us on that account: what does it matter! They will say: "Their *honesty* – that is their devilry, and nothing else!" What does it matter! And even if they were right – have not all Gods hitherto been such sanctified, re-baptized devils?"[295]

The image of the knight accompanied by death and the devil in Albrecht Dürer's work was still alive in Nietzsche's spirit of when he wrote the last pages of *Ecce Homo*. He quoted a passage from *Thus Spoke Zarathustra* in which the *superman* is the *devil* to a certain extent: "You highest men my eyes have encountered! This is my doubt of you and my secret laughter: I think you would call my superman – a devil! Your souls are so unfamiliar with what is great that the superman would be fearful to you

---

293   Friedrich Nietzsche, *The Gay Science*, 2006, p. 41.
294   Ibidem, p. 227.
295   Friedrich Nietzsche, *Beyond Good and Evil*, available at https://www.gutenberg.org/ebooks/4363. Accessed February 28, 2016.

in his goodness".[296] Friedrich Nietzsche's commentary on his own text can be summed up in a single principle: the devil, as the symbol of evil, is itself a matter of the interpretation or perspective of the person making a value judgement. For most researchers, Napoleon was a diabolical man, but for Nietzsche he was highly close to being a *superman*. Also, Cesare Borgia, who is remembered in history as a devil with a human face, falls, from Friedrich Nietzsche's perspective, into the category of the *superman*, as he said in *Ecce Homo*.

The association of Cesare Borgia with the *superman* is, today, more than then, unfavourable to Friedrich Nietzsche. Who could take seriously a philosopher who makes of an unscrupulous assassin a superhuman character, capable of giving meaning to the future history of humanity? But the image that Nietzsche had made of Cesare Borgia owes a lot to Machiavelli, in whose *Il Principe* he appeared as a model politician of the era. With well-known realism, Machiavelli, in chapter VII of his work *The Prince*, did not overlook Cesare Borgia's cruelty, cunning and many vices, but, because all these were used to achieve some lofty goals, he is presented as an exemplary politician. Machiavelli did not find fault with him: on the contrary, he presented him as a model of what Nietzsche would later call the man of the will to power. As a historical figure, Cesare Borgia was for Friedrich Nietzsche a typical Renaissance man. Like any exceptional politician, he was possessed by the *demon of power*, a phenomenon described in *The Dawn of Day* as follows: "Neither necessity nor desire, but the love of power is the demon of mankind. You may give men everything possible – health, food, shelter, enjoyment – but they are and remain unhappy and capricious for the demon waits and waits; and must be satisfied. Let everything else be taken away from men and let this demon be satisfied and then they will nearly be happy – as happy as men and demons can be".[297]

Friedrich Nietzsche invokes Cesare Borgia, Napoleon and other similar historical figures to exemplify his axiological thesis according to which the

---

296 Friedrich Nietzsche, *Ecce Homo*, available at https://archive.org/details/TheCompleteWorksOfFriedrichNietzschevol.17-EcceHomo. Accessed February 28, 2016.

297 Friedrich Nietzsche, *The Dawn of Day*, available at http://www.gutenberg.org/files/39955/39955-h/39955-h.html. Accessed February 28, 2016.

will to power is ultimately the standard of all values. It would be unfair to believe that Nietzsche idealized tyrants; on the contrary, in the spirit of Machiavelli, he is a realist who distinguishes strongly between the reputation of a character, built mostly artificially with a kind of machine that produces glory, and his ruthless opponents or fanatic followers. The reputation accorded to Cesare Borgia in history is unfair in the sense that the interpreters of his actions have exaggerated the monstrous features of his personality, overshadowing the positive ones, and totally neglecting the extremely unfavourable historical circumstances in which he conducted his political life and work. What Friedrich Nietzsche particularly wanted to point out when he tried to illustrate his theory of the superman with the example of Cesare Borgia was the will to power as an objective standard of values. Given the lucidity that he acquired studying Machiavelli's *The Prince*, he did not ignore the *evil* which such characters possessed by the demon of power leave behind them, but he distinguished between *the evil that comes from power* and that which originates from *weakness*. The latter is perverse, always manifests itself in the guise of good, and seduces by looking like poisonous but beautifully coloured mushrooms. "This evil of strength wounds others unintentionally – it must find an outlet somewhere; while the evil of weakness wishes to wound and to see signs of suffering".[298] The historical examples of superman that are found in the works of Friedrich Nietzsche support the idea of the will to power as on axiological standard. Values and non-values are distinguished according to this criterion. The will to power is direct, brutal, natural, and produced openly, honestly. Therefore, it does not stop being evil, but, unlike the evil that comes from weakness, it is, if one may say so, an evil assumed. The same thing happens with goodness and all other values. For instance, *generosity* is a positive value in most civilizations, but, for Friedrich Nietzsche, there is a big difference between offering another person some of your property because this is what your own nature dictates, which is the same thing as the will to power, and that *generosity* that arises from weakness and fear. The same goes for *hospitality*, to cite another example of the many offered by Friedrich Nietzsche throughout his work. It is also recognized as

---

298 Ibidem.

a positive value in most civilizations, but it makes a big difference whether the *hospitality* comes from the will to power or from *weakness*, even if its immediate effects are the same. "The object of hospitality is to paralyse all hostile feeling in a stranger. When we cease to look upon strangers as enemies, hospitality diminishes; it flourishes so long as its evil presupposition does".[299] Obviously, today we do not question the *intention* of the benefactor, or the value of his gesture: we take into account only the results of his beneficence. But, for Friedrich Nietzsche, the source of value is important to the appropriate assessment of its validity. The principle of his axiology in this regard is as follows: everything that comes from the will to power, no matter how evil it is, is better than anything that comes from weakness. At its limit, it can be said that hatred of the powerful, in the Nietzschean sense of the term, is worthier than petty love of the weak.

---

299   Ibidem.

Bibliography

Arendt, Dieter (ed.), *Der Nihilismus als Phänomen der Geistesgeschichte in der wissenschaftlichen Diskussion unseres Jahrhunderts* (Darmstadt: Wissenschaftliche Buchgesellschaft, 1974).

Benn, Gottfried, *Nietzsche – Nach fünfzig Jahren* in *Essays, Reden, Vorträge* (Wiesbaden: Limes Verlag, 1962).

Benz, Ernst, *Der Übermensch* (Zürich/Stuttgart: Rhein-Verlag, 1961).

Bertram, Ernst, *Nietzsche. Încercare de mitologie* (Bucureşti: Editura Humanitas, 1998).

Bühler, Axel (ed.): *Unzeitgemässe Hermeneutik: Verstehen und Interpretation im Denken der Aufklärung* (Frankfurt am Main: Vittorio Klostermann, 1994).

Challemel-Lacour, P., *Études et réflexions d'un pessimiste*, (Paris: Charpentier, 1901).

Dieterich, Anton, *Miguel de Cervantes. Mit Selbstzeugnissen und Bilddokumenten* (Hamburg: Rowohlt Verlag, 1984).

Dilthey, Wilhelm, *Leben Schleiermachers*, in *Gesammelte Schriften*, Band XIV (Göttingen: Verlag Vandenhoeck & Ruprecht, 1966).

Flacius, Matthias, *Über den Erkenntnisgrund der Heiligen Schrift*, übersetzt von Lutz Geldsetzer (Düsseldorf: Janssen Verlag, 1968).

Gawoll, Hans-Jürgen, *Nihilismus und Metaphysik. Entwicklungsgeschichtliche Untersuchung vom deutschen Idealismus bis zu Heidegger* (Stuttgart: Frommann-Holzboog Verlag, 1989).

Gisela Deesz, *Die Entwicklung des Nietzsche-Bildes in Deutschland* (Würzburg: Triltsch Verlag, 1933).

Hartmann, Nicolai, *Ethics*, Vol. II (London/New York: Allen & Macmillan Company, 1932).

Herder, Johann Gottfried, *Ideen zur Philosophie der Geschichte der Menschheit*, (Wiesbaden: Löwit-Verlag, 1966).

Hermann L. Goldschmidt, *Der Nihilismus im Licht einer kritischen Philosophie* (Frankfurt am Main: Europäische Verlagsanstalt, 1941).

Kant, Immanuel, *Die Metaphysik der Sitten* (Berlin: Verlag von L. Heimann, 1870).

Köster, Peter, *Der verbotene Philosoph: Studien zu den Anfängen der katholischen Nietzsche-Rezeption in Deutschland (1890–1918)* (Berlin: Walter de Gruyter, 1998).

Kraus, Wolfgang, *Nihilismus heute oder die Geduld der Weltgeschichte* (Wien/Hamburg: Zsolnay Verlag, 1983).

Leis, Mario, *Frauen um Nietzsche* (Hamburg: Rowolt Verlag, 2000).

Leist, Fritz, *Existenz im Nichts. Versuch einer Analyse des Nihilismus* (München: Manz Verlag, 1961).

Lessing, Theodor, *Nietzsche* (Berlin: Ullstein Verlag, 1925).

Marroni, Aldo, *L'enigma dell'impuro. La sfida dell'estetico nella società, nella sessualità e nell'arte* (Roma: Carocci editore, 2007).

Meier, Georg Friedrich, *Versuch einer allgemeinen Auslegungskunst* (Düsseldorf: Stern-Verlag, 1965).

Meysenbug, Malwida von, *Memorien einer Idealistin* (Berlin/Leipzig: Schuster & Loeffler Verlag, 1903).

Montinari, Mazzino, *Nietzsche, Friedrich. Eine Einführung* (Berlin: Walter de Gruyter, 1991).

Neumeister, Sebastien, "Der romantische Don Quijote", in *Miguel de Cervantes' Don Quijote. Explizite und implizite Diskurse im "Don Quijote"*, ed. Christoph Strosetzki (Berlin: Schmidt Verlag, 2005).

Nietzsche, Friedrich, *Der Wille zur Macht: Versuch einer Umwertung aller Werte* (Stuttgart: Kröner Verlag, 1964).

Nietzsche, Friedrich, *Die Geburt der Tragödie aus dem Geiste der Musik* (Frankfurt am Main: Insel Verlag, 2000).

Nietzsche, Friedrich, *Götzendämmerung. Der Antichrist. Ecce homo. Gedichte* (Stuttgart: Kröner Verlag, 1954).

Nietzsche, Friedrich, *Human, All Too Human: A Book for Free Spirits*, trans. Marion Faber (Nebraska: University of Nebraska Press, 1996).

Nietzsche, Friedrich, *Jenseits von Gut und Böse* (Frankfurt am Main: Insel Verlag, 1986).

Nietzsche, Friedrich, *Morgenröte. Gedanken über die moralischen Vorurteile* (Stuttgart, Kröner Verlag, 1939).

Nietzsche, Friedrich, *On the Genealogy of Morals*, trans. Douglas Smith (Oxford: Oxford University Press, 2008).

Nietzsche, Friedrich, *The Anti-Christ*, trans. R. J. Hollingdale (New York: Penguin Books, 2003).

Nietzsche, Friedrich, *The Gay Science*, trans. Josefine Nauckhoff (Cambridge: Cambridge University Press, 2001).

Nietzsche, Friedrich, *Thoughts Out of Season*, trans. Anthony M. Ludovici (Edinburgh: The Edinburgh Press, 1909).

Nietzsche, Friedrich, *Thus Spoke Zarathustra*: A Book for Everyone and Nobody, trans. Graham Parkes (Oxford: Oxford University Press, 2008).

Nietzsche, Friedrich, *Twilight of the Idols*, trans. R. J. Hollingdale (New York: Penguin Books, 2003).

Nordau, Max, *Entartung* I/II (Berlin: Duncker Verlag, 1892/93).

Papini, Giovani, *Amurgul filosofilor* (București: Editura Uranus, 1991).

Pisa, Karl, *Schopenhauer. Kronzeuge einer unheilen Welt* (Berlin: Paul Neff Verlag, 1977).

Râmbu, Nicolae, "Two axiological illnesses", *Journal of Human Values*, 21.2 (2015): 64–71.

Rauschning, Hermann, *Masken und Metamorfosen des Nihilismus*, Frankfurt am Main/Wien: Humboldt-Verlag, 1954).

Riel, Alexander, *Zum 200. Geburtstag Arthur Schopenhauers. Briefe im Interesse seiner Philosophie* (München: Verlag Besold, 1988).

Scheler, Max, *Omul resentimentului* (București: Editura Humanitas, 2007).

Schleiermacher, F.D.E, *Hermeneutik und Kritik*, (Frankfurt am Main: Suhrkamp Verlag, 1995).

Schopenhauer, Arthur, *Gesammelte Briefe* (Bonn: Bouvier Verlag, 1987).

Schopenhauer, Arthur, *Parerga und Paralipomena* (Zürich: Haffmans Verlag, 1991).

Schopenhauer, Arthur, *The Wisdom of Life and other Essays*, trans. Bailey Saunders and Ernest Belfort Bax (Washington & London: M. Walter Dunne, 1901).

Schopenhauer, Arthur, *The World as Will and Idea*, trans. R. B. Haldane and J. Kemp (London: Kegan Paul, Trench, Trübner & Co., 1909).

Seubold, Günter and Baum, Patrick (eds.), *Was mir Nietzsche bedeutet* (Bonn: DenkMal Verlag, 2001).

Thielicke, Helmut, *Der Nihilismus. Entstehung, Wesen, Überwindung* (Tübingen: Reichl Verlag, 1950).

Türck, Hermann, *Omul genial* (Bucureşti: Editura Socec, 1898).

Unamuno, Miguel de, "Ideocraţia", in *Eseişti spanioli* (Bucureşti: Editura Univers, 1982).

Valadier, Paul, "L'anarchie des valeurs", *Cultura: International Journal of Philosophy of Culture and Axiology*, 3/1 (2006): 89–100.

Verrecchia, Anacleto, *Zarathustras Ende. Die Katastrophe Nietzsches in Turin* (Wien: Böhlaus Verlag, 1986).

Volkelt, Johannes, *Arthur Schopenhauer. Seine Persönlichkeit, seine Lehre, sein Glaube* (Sturttgart: Frommanns Verlag, 1901).

www.ingramcontent.com/pod-product-compliance
Lightning Source LLC
Chambersburg PA
CBHW030919150426
42812CB00046B/353